The Best Baby Shower Book

A Complete Guide for Party Planners

Courtney Cooke

Meadowbrook
Distributed by Simon & Schuster
New York

Library of Congress Cataloging-In-Publication Data

Cooke, Courtney
    The best baby shower book.

    1. Showers (Parties)—planning. 2. Infants.—
I. Title.
GV1472.7.S5C66 1986 793.2 86-12440
ISBN 0-88166-081-5 (pbk.)
ISBN 0-671-62276-5 (Simon & Schuster : pbk.)

Published by Meadowbrook, Inc., 18318 Minnetonka Boulevard, Deephaven, MN 55391

BOOK TRADE DISTRIBUTION by Simon and Schuster, a division of Simon & Schuster, Inc., 1230 Avenue of the Americas, New York, NY 10020.

S&S Ordering # 0-671-62276-5 (Priced)
                 0-671-62281-1 (Unpriced)

86 87 88 89 10 9 8 7 6 5 4 3 2
Printed in the United States of America.

Editorial Director: Bruce Lansky
Editor: Margaret Liddiard
Copy Editor/Writer: Sara Saetre
Researcher/Writer: Christine Larsen, Barb DeGroot
Art Direction: Nancy MacLean
Text Design: Lynda Lawson, Jill Rogers
Cover Design: Nancy MacLean, April Grande
Illustrator: April Grande
Keyline: Mike Tuminelly
Production: John Howard

Baby talk definitions on page 60 of Chapter 4 were excerpted from *Baby Talk,* a book by Bruce Lansky © Copyright 1986, with permission of its publisher, Meadowbrook, Inc.

Humorous "laws" on page 59 of Chapter 4 were excerpted from *Mother Murphy's Law,* a book by Bruce Lansky © Copyright 1986, with permission of its publisher, Meadowbrook, Inc.

The cartoons on pages 116 through 118 of the Appendix were excerpted from *"Hi Mom! Hi Dad!"* by Lynn Johnston © Copyright 1977, with permission of its publisher, Meadowbrook, Inc.

Table of Contents

Acknowledgments

We would like to thank all of the people who answered our questionnaires and, in particular, the following people, without whose input the book would not have been complete: Diane Camp, Lori Carleton, Carol Cook, Dorothy Cook, Mary Curran, Barbara DeGroot, Colleen Finochiaro, Elaine Fong, Elizabeth Foyt, Karen Hamilton, Shannon Jahnke, Betty Lundquist, Lynn Miller, Minnetonka Lutheran Nursery School, Dorothy Stuber, and Barbara Unell.

Introduction

Get ready for this . . . . baby showers can be fun! You may remember the typical baby shower as trivial and silly (at best) or as embarrassing and beastly dull (at worst). But it doesn't have to be that way. Babies are still a reason to celebrate. And new parents need the fun and practical gifts given to them at showers. We can continue to celebrate with a shower without continuing those traditions that have lost meaning. Our celebrations—our baby showers—can be as exuberant, as alive, and as much fun as we are.

Childbirth and parenthood have changed drastically over the last 20 years. Fathers increasingly are involved in the birth of their babies. They attend childbirth classes, help in the delivery room, and take a much more active role in the care of their new babies than their fathers and grandfathers did. Some new fathers even take over the primary caretaking of their children while the mothers return to work.

Despite the changes, baby showers have remained fundamentally the same. They don't reflect the emerging equality between the sexes; fathers are often left out completely. There are still times when women only will want to gather to support a pregnant friend, but at other times, it may be equally appropriate to include men.

Many baby showers also fail to reflect today's emphasis on nutrition, serving up menus that seem like a sugary, salty, fatty attack on efforts to eat wholesome, low-calorie foods. Traditional shower foods are often difficult to eat, too, when balanced on guests' laps. You can serve foods that are easy to eat and that your guests can enjoy at any party.

The old-fashioned shower games have to go. They often seem intended to halt activity, conversation—and spontaneous fun. Instead, you can provide activities that really will entertain your guests. Or leave them free to simply entertain themselves.

Finally, yesterday's shower often assumed that women were free to attend at any time and that the hostess had ample time to putter with elaborate decorations and foods. But today neither hosts (male and female) nor guests may want to spend hours planning and attending a baby shower. Both may be working full-time or squeezing a shower into an otherwise busy schedule. And that's okay. Giving a baby shower can be as simple as inviting the mother-to-be's work colleagues to lunch. A shower should reflect your schedule and that of the new parents and your guests. It certainly needn't be an elaborate, inconvenient affair.

So you don't need to hesitate to throw a baby shower, just forget the stodgy routines of the showers you shudder to remember. Enjoy yourself. There are many new ways to celebrate the birth of a child. The best way is with a party.

The Best Baby Shower Book shows how. We've included many practical suggestions for organizing a streamlined, but lively, shower. Use them to carefully organize a party around a theme or to discover shortcuts for fitting the shower into your busy schedule. Many of the activities will be welcome replacements for traditional icebreaker games. And many will be enjoyed equally by men and women.

The book also contains ample menu suggestions for foods that are delicious as well as easy to prepare, serve, and eat. And, best of all, they are more nutritious than party foods you're familiar with. There are recipes for snacks, appetizers, main dishes, salads, desserts and beverages . . . some that include alcohol, and many that don't.

We've also pioneered a new concept in baby showers: The party is the present. It's a practical approach—the party's theme or activities result in a really useful gift for the new parents. The suggested prizes for guests, the decorating ideas, and the "wish list" the expectant parents can complete are also very practical. These will help you eliminate silly, wasteful decorations and party prizes. Finally, we've included blank pages for your own ideas. Everything you need to plan a successful shower is here, in one handy place.

A baby shower ought to be fun. You don't need to settle for the kind of shower you used to hate. You *can* plan a shower you and your friends will genuinely enjoy, and one that will communicate your support and confidence in the new parents. This book will show you how.

Why Give a Baby Shower?

No one seems to know just where or when baby showers began. Bridal showers were popular in the United States as early as 1900, but baby showers as we know them today did not become commonplace until shortly after World War II—possibly the first manifestation of the baby boom. Prior to that time, gift-giving to new parents was usually more of an informal event—a hand-made gift for baby's layette, given after the baby was born.

Baby showers have always filled several basic needs. They help the new parents acquire things a baby needs, which might otherwise drain the family budget. Baby showers also provide emotional support for an expectant couple who may be facing some anxiety about their new roles. And baby showers are ideal for celebrating the birth of a child—marking the passage of an important stage of life. Finally, they can be just plain fun!

Celebrating Every Baby

Remember: Baby showers aren't just for first-time parents. Every baby deserves a special welcome by parents' family, friends and co-workers. As a matter of fact, the more children already in a family, the more the expectant parents will enjoy a baby shower; updating the requisite supply of baby necessities is always practical. Just as important is the sharing of the joy every baby adds to a family.

Chapter One **Planning a Shower**

Whether you're thinking of hosting a large gathering with a substantial menu (catered by you!)—or a Saturday morning get-together with a few close friends and a cup of coffee, do take some time to plan your party, whatever its scope. Even the simplest gathering will lose its charm if an important detail (such as inviting the new parents) is forgotten.

Setting the Date

Your first step will be to set a date. Contact the parents-to-be before you settle on one; their schedules will be your first consideration. They may also be able to help you anticipate any scheduling difficulties for the shower guests.

You can hold your shower either before the baby is born or after: both times have advantages. Parents expecting their first child may need many of the basics. By holding their shower in advance (usually three to six weeks before the baby is due), you give them some time to get organized. And since the last weeks of a pregnancy can be trying, a shower during that time can provide valuable emotional support.

If you hold the shower after the baby is born, you'll have the advantage of knowing the baby's sex. Guests can purchase "fun" clothing intended just for boys or girls. They can make personalized gifts if they wish, and guess sizes better. You also set the stage for an appearance by the *real* guest of honor—the baby!

Allow yourself plenty of time. You should contact the parents-to-be to set a date for the party at least two months before the due date if you are planning to hold the event before the baby is born.

Invite guests at least two weeks before the party, to give them ample time to arrange their schedules. And remember, a baby shower is one party for which *guests* must prepare—they'll want to shop for a gift. Mail the invitations even earlier if you're planning an "after-the-birthday" party. Otherwise, the people you're inviting might plan an affair of their own!

Guest List

Once you've set the shower date, you can determine your guest list. You may already have a list in mind (family members, work colleagues, neighbors, club members or members of another group). Or the expectant parents themselves may provide you with a list.

The invitations you send might reflect the theme of your party, if you choose one. You can simply write them on notepaper or buy special baby shower invitations. You may want to include gift information in the invitation (see the "Gifts" section). Be sure to include your name, phone number, and address.

You'll want to know the number of guests attending, even for a casual party. You can handle the response in two ways: list R.S.V.P. and everyone will be obligated to reply; or write "Regrets Only" by your phone number and only those who can't make it need respond.

Do's and Don't's

1. **Do** plan ahead; get your invitations out as early as possible.

2. **Do** take time before the party to get organized so that it will run smoothly. Then you'll have time to enjoy it, too.

3. **Do** consider including men.

4. **Do** have fun with festive decorations. Consider useful decorations and centerpieces that can be given to the guest or guests of honor at the end of the party.

5. **Do** use your best table linens and silver if the party isn't too big. Save the matching paper plate ensembles for larger parties or when you just don't have time to wash linens and china.

6. **Do** present foods attractively; include festive garnishes.

7. **Do** know the diet restrictions of your group, especially those of the mother-to-be. If you plan to serve alcoholic beverages, label them clearly.

8. **Do** serve foods that are easy to eat.

9. **Don't** expect people to balance a sit-down meal on their laps.

10. **Do** have one or two very organized people sitting near the mother (or mother and father) to handle wrappings and to record the gifts received.

11. **Don't** give all newborn or three-month size clothing; the baby will soon wear larger sizes.

12. **Do** include the mother and father when buying gifts—a personal gift for the parents during this stressful time can give them a real lift.

13. **Do** keep the shower short and sweet.

14. **Don't** play games that are embarrassing or awkward for your guests.

15. **Do** include really useful prizes for guests.

16. Finally, **do** have a good time!

Checklist

Use this checklist as a general guide to the many details you'll want to consider when planning your shower. You may even want to photocopy it and actually check each step as you complete it. Adjust it as necessary for your own situation. Some items may not apply. For example, if you will hold a potluck dinner shower, you *won't* need to prepare a grocery list! On the other hand, you may want to add information. If you need to borrow three fondue pots, two card tables and a punch bowl, you may want to list them and check them off as you acquire them.

Two months before the baby's due date
☐ Call expectant mother or father

Three weeks before the party
☐ Set guest list
☐ Set time, date
☐ Choose theme (optional)
☐ Make or purchase invitations

Two-three weeks before the party
☐ Send invitations
☐ Plan menu
☐ Plan activities and prizes (optional)
☐ Decide on your shower gift (allow more time if you will make it)
☐ Coordinate the purchase of a group gift (optional)

One-two weeks before the party
☐ Make or purchase decorations
☐ Purchase gift
☐ Wrap gift (so you don't forget and leave this to the last minute!)
☐ Prepare shopping list for all menu ingredients

One week before the party	☐ Have serving dishes and utensils ready (you may need to borrow some)
	☐ Make sure folding tables and chairs are handy and in good repair (you may need to borrow these, too)
	☐ Wash and iron table linens, if necessary
	☐ Check R.S.V.P.'s to determine number of guests
	☐ Call expectant mother and/or father to remind them of shower
Three days before the party	☐ Buy groceries (except fresh bread or rolls)
	☐ Order centerpiece and other fresh flowers (optional)
	☐ Clean house
The day before the party	☐ Prepare as much of menu as possible
	☐ Set table
	☐ Set up folding tables and chairs, if possible
	☐ Assemble paraphernalia for activities
	☐ Wrap prizes (optional)
	☐ Wrap gift, if you haven't already
The day of the party	☐ Dust and vacuum
	☐ Cut flowers and arrange centerpiece, if you're creating your own
	☐ Pick up flowers, if you're buying them
	☐ Arrange balloons, streamers or other festive decorations (optional)
	☐ Buy fresh bread, rolls
	☐ Set out coasters and ashtrays
	☐ Prepare the rest of menu
Last-minute details	☐ Get dressed at least one-half to one hour before you expect the first guests (You don't want to be surprised by an early arrival!)
	☐ Have coffee ready to brew and other beverages ready
	☐ Greet first guests
	☐ Have a good time!

Tip: It's a good idea to make a detailed list of each item you plan to serve (including butter, rolls, beverages and garnishes) and post this list in a conspicuous spot in your kitchen. Then you can check each item off as you prepare it and again as you serve it. This way, you can avoid forgetting important items.

Chapter Two # Choosing a Theme

Consider choosing a theme for your party. Though you may think a theme will make more work for you, it can actually be a time-saver because it provides a focus for the party. A theme can also make your party more festive. Invitations, decorations, activities and even foods can be planned around the central theme.

A theme is, of course, optional. Parties can be just as successful without one and your group may be the sort that prefers a spontaneous party.

In this chapter we've included a number of ideas that can be used with or without a theme. Choose what works best for you.

If you prefer to use a theme, there are many possibilities. The best themes are often the simplest. One easy approach is to plan around any traditional symbol of a new baby. Try variations on diapers, storks, pink-and-blue, teddy bears, cradles, trees, and. . .well, let your imagination be your guide.

Or, you can choose one of the themes below. It's not necessary to spend lots of money on invitations and decorations. The cleverest ones are those you make yourself—we've provided plenty of suggestions. Included are ideas for invitations, name tags, centerpieces, table settings, gifts, decorations, and even seats of honor.

A seat of honor is a chair set aside for the mother-to-be. If you have included men, you may want to reserve a seat for the father-to-be also. You can decorate these "thrones" to make the new parents feel extra-special. Select sturdy chairs in which the guests of honor can see and talk to other guests easily, and where guests can easily see the presents being opened. If the new mother is very pregnant, select a chair in which she will be comfortable. (Low, overstuffed chairs are difficult for pregnant women to get into and out of comfortably and gracefully.)

Diapers

Invitations Cut a piece of stationery and fold to resemble a tri-fold diaper. (See Appendix.) Write the shower information inside. Then fold and fasten with a tiny gold safety pin. Or, begin with a piece of white or pastel flannel and fold it. Write the shower information on a notecard. (A three-by-five inch card in a pastel color is a good choice.) Insert the card in the "diaper."

Name tags Fold a triangle of white or pastel construction paper in the shape of a diaper, and fasten with a small, gold safety pin. (See Appendix.) Guests write their names on the outside and use the safety pin to attach the tag. If you wish, put a small dab of mustard inside one or several of the "diapers." Guests who draw a dirty diaper win a door prize.

Centerpiece Fold a piece of felt or flannel around a bowl and fasten with hand-painted or animal-shaped diaper pins. Arrange flowers in the bowl. Give the diaper pins— or the entire arrangement—to the guest of honor after the party. Or "diaper" a blooming fresh plant and give it to the guests of honor.

Table setting Tie a white or pastel linen napkin around silver settings in a tri-fold "diaper."

Storks

Invitations   Trace the stork shape (see Appendix) from pink stationery and write shower information on the front. Or, fold the stationery before tracing to make a card and write the information inside. You can buy bulk stationery from many stationers, or in the stationery departments of some department stores. (See the Appendix for directions for making your own cards.)

Name tags   Trace stork outline and cut it out of the same stationery you used for the invitations, or use white or pastel construction paper.

Table setting   Stork centerpieces are generally available in gift and card shops. Wrap a napkin around silver settings and tie with a ribbon; attach a plastic or paper stork.

Seat of honor   Attach stork cutouts and balloons to the chair. Twist paper streamers from the wall or ceiling to the chair.

Teddy Bears

Invitations   Use notepaper with teddy bears (available in the children's department). Or, add teddy bear stickers or trace or photocopy the bear (see Appendix) onto blank notepaper. Commercial invitations with darling teddy bears are also available.

Name tags   Trace or photocopy the bear outline (see Appendix) on tan or pastel construction paper. Add ribbon bow ties and draw dots for eyes and nose.

Table setting   Apply teddy bear stickers to the centerpiece vase. Place little stuffed bears (find them at a dime store or toy department) here and there on the table.

Seat of honor   Attach a balloon bouquet above the chair; hang a paper bear on ribbon streamers from the balloons. Tuck real teddy bears by the chair and around the room. One of the bears could be your gift to the new parents.

Cradles

Invitations   Trace the outline of a baby in a cradle (see Appendix) on construction paper and cut it out. Write your shower information on the cradle.

Name tags   Trace or photocopy the cradle in the Appendix. Add a baby's face and a piece of fabric for a quilt.

Decorating hint   If you have a real or toy cradle (or bassinette or carriage), decorate it with ribbons and balloons. Then use it to hold the gifts before they are opened. If you don't have a cradle, make one from a cardboard box and cover it with giftwrap.

Trees

Invitations   On blank stationery, trace or photocopy the outline of a tree (see Appendix). Draw little circles on it, as in a family tree. Insert the shower information in the circles. Photocopy the tree and mount the copies on colored stationery.

Name tags   Trace or photocopy the leaf shape (see Appendix) and cut it out of colored construction paper. Or, cut twigs from a tree or bush and tie a circle of paper to them with a ribbon.

Centerpiece   This arrangement will be most effective in the spring. Weight a pitcher or vase with sand or marbles. Insert small branches from an ornamental or flowering tree. Hang tiny baby items on the tree: cute diaper pins, rattles, booties, baby jewelry, and hair ribbons (if the baby is a girl). These items can be given to the new parents.

Gift idea   Furnish a live fruit tree or ornamental tree in a pot. As guests bring their gifts, attach the small ones to the tree's branches and arrange the large ones around the tree's base. After the other gifts have been opened, present the tree to the new parents. They may want to plant it as a lasting memento of their baby's birth. (See Traditions from Around the World, page 85).

Little Cowboy

This theme is especially fun for a couples shower. Guests might like to come wearing cowboy hats, boots, and jeans to welcome the new little "pardner." You might hold the shower in your backyard and end it with a barbecue.

Invitations Cut a cowboy hat from tan paper (see outline in the Appendix); mount it on white, folded notepapers. Add a piece of ribbon for a hatband. Write shower information on the inside.

Name tags Cut out cowboy hats and write names on them.

Centerpiece Set a child's cowboy hat on the table upside down. Place a bowl with fresh, dried or silk flowers in it. Or insert a green plant in it and give it to the parents-to-be after the shower.

Gift ideas A pair of denim overalls with a bandana "bib" would be an ideal gift. A rocking horse would be a great group gift.

Activity It is a custom in Texas to give new parents a piggy bank that guests have filled with money.

The Twins Party

If the mother-to-be is expecting twins, consider a shower using twins as a theme. A baby shower for a couple expecting twins is sure to be welcome. And it's appropriate even if the couple has older children; there are so many things they're sure to need in multiples.

Invitations Cut a baby outline from a folded piece of stationery (see Appendix); unfold (like a string of paper dolls) and write the shower information on the inside. Decorate the front to look like a baby, or write a message like "It's going to be *twins*!"

Name tags   Trace or photocopy the design provided in the Appendix.

Centerpiece   Cut a string of paper dolls from colored paper, in a shade to match your table scheme. If the babies already have been born, choose an outline that is obviously a girl or a boy. (If the parents got one of each, cut a string of each.) Stand the string of dolls in a circle around a bowl of flowers.

Gift ideas   Following are some things that are especially needed by parents of twins:

Certificates

An offer of help is greatly appreciated by the overworked parents of twins. Consider certificates for help with meals, babysitting or even driving. (It's hard enough to load *one* baby in the car for a doctor's appointment, let alone *two!*)

Equipment

Pool resources with other guests to provide a "big ticket" item: an extra car seat, double or extra swing, play equipment for the yard, extra crib, high chair or double stroller. (Note: side-by-side strollers don't fit through doorways!) Parents of twins may be strapped for funds and could use a helping hand here. Keep in mind that much of this equipment will receive double use, so quality and durability (and safety!) are extra important.

Clothing

Essentially, every piece of clothing (including and especially shoes) is needed in duplicate. The harried parents of two babies are less likely to have time for frequent clothes washing, so *more than double* the amount of clothing is really required! Many guests won't want to buy two of the same thing, so consider "pairing" guests to buy duplicates of items they select. Some sensitivity is required here, however. Guests may not want to be paired. And some parents wouldn't dream of dressing their babies alike, while others can't wait. Find out first what the parents—and your guests—prefer.

Diaper service

Purchasing disposable diapers for two babies is expensive and washing the reusable kind takes time that parents of twins may not have. A diaper service can be a very welcome gift!

Twins Magazine

A subscription to this magazine would be especially useful before the babies are born, so the parents have time to read it! *Twins Magazine* provides valuable information about parenting twins, as well as emotional support. (See Books and Magazines, page 73.)

Individual picture frames

Having separate pictures helps each twin foster a healthy self-image.

A blank book

A blank book (perhaps one covered with pretty printed fabric) can be a great help to the harried parents of twins. They can use it to keep track of their babies' schedules (who eats first, who naps longer, etc.) and preferences. The book can also be invaluable to babysitters and other helpers who don't want to ask questions constantly. And later, after the children have passed a stage, the parents may enjoy looking back and seeing—in detail—all that has happened. The parents may even want to record daily observations, if they have time.

Other gifts Many parents of twins struggle just to provide the basics for their children. They may appreciate a "frivolous" gift for their little ones even more than other parents would, since it's unlikely they'll be able to purchase these things themselves. Consider buying one or two special outfits. If you can't afford to buy two, buy one and "pair up" with someone else who wants to buy a corresponding gift. Buying two toys—a different one for each child—is also a great idea. Twins do so much sharing, each needs to own something, even at a very young age.

The Family Party

Families usually can be counted on for major financial and emotional support for new mothers and fathers. The family party calls them together to honor the new parents and provide them with a substantial part of the needed items for the new baby. This type of party is an excellent opportunity to involve the brothers, uncles, sons, and nephews.

Invitations You may simply want to call family members with your invitations. Otherwise, use the "family tree" invitation idea on page 101.

Name tags While name tags aren't usually necessary for a family party, you may want to provide them if you are combining several branches of a family and some members may not know each other. Use the "family tree" name tag on page 102.

Centerpiece Try to assemble small baby pictures of all the people in your family (or at least those of family members who will attend the shower). Protect the pictures by mounting them in lightweight, miniature frames. Weight a large vase or bowl with sand or pebbles. Gather small tree branches. (Spray them white or pastel colors for a more festive look.) Arrange the twigs in your container, and hang the baby pictures from them with pink and blue ribbons. Your guests will enjoy remembering their relatives as babies or guessing their identities.

Activity Now's the time to bring out your old home movies or snapshots of the new parents, if you have them. Showing the movies and photos is especially fun if both of the new parents are represented. Your family may enjoy discussing what the new parents were like as babies and as children, then predicting what the new baby will be like. (See Activities Chapter.)

The "Block" Party

If your neighborhood is closely knit, this can be great fun. The "block" party is also ideal for including men or entire families and would make a terrific surprise party. Schedule an outdoor barbecue if the weather permits. If there are small children attending, be sure to line up some appropriate activities or have some of the teenagers keep an eye on them. Notify all but the guests of honor that the theme of this party is a baby shower for the "Smiths." Be sure to assign an essential job to the Smiths to guarantee their attendance.

Invitations Draw on the idea of a neighborhood "grapevine" in one of two ways. Deliver your invitation through the "grapevine" by phone or over the back fence. Or, copy the grapevine design in the Appendix on stationery, together with the shower information and mail or hand-deliver the invitations.

Name tags If your neighborhood is friendly enough for a baby shower, you probably won't need name tags. But if there are new families who will attend, you may want to use them. Use the grapevine design shown in the Appendix.

Centerpiece Since this is a "block" party, create a focal point using colorful wooden blocks.

Food This is the easiest part—a pot luck dinner is perfect!

The Office Party

An office party can be fun, if the co-workers are close and enjoy each other's company. (This is also a great occasion for a surprise party.) A few special considerations apply when you plan this type of party. You'll want to schedule a convenient time and place for your colleagues—perhaps a long lunch in a restaurant near work or in the company break room. An evening get-together in your home may be convenient, if people don't have to travel too far from home. If you live far from the office, consider scheduling the shower right after work to save your co-workers some traveling back and forth. But a shower after work means you're faced with company the minute you walk in your door—consider the pros and cons.

Guest list

Women in an office are the traditional participants in a gathering of this kind, but that's changing. Don't automatically discount the men. Especially if you're planning a low-key lunch, the men in your office might enjoy a chance to join the fun.

Invitations

Circulate a "memo" to any "interested parties," notifying them of the purpose, date, time, and location of the event (see Appendix). In this way, work associates who don't want to take part will know they weren't forgotten, but won't feel pressured to buy a shower gift.

If you prefer individual invitations, make up "message slips" with the shower information on them, and deliver them. See the Appendix for appropriate forms.

Name tags

The people at your gathering will probably know each other. But if some come from different departments or branches and aren't acquainted, do provide name tags. Use the stick-on name tags used at conventions and seminars.

Gift idea

Since working people may not have much time for shopping and also may not be sure what to buy, consider a group gift for the office shower. Ask for a donation of a set amount of money. Or request a donation to a "kitty," which you or a committee will use to buy one large gift or a collection of smaller gifts.

Pink-and-Blue

This theme is ideal for honoring a baby who is already born. You'll know which color to emphasize!

Invitations   These can be as simple as blue ink on pink stationery. Add cute stickers or drawn designs, if you're inclined. Or, trace the designs shown for the name tag game in the Appendix.

Name tags   Again, try blue ink on a simple pink tag.

Centerpiece   Arrange a centerpiece of pink and blue flowers and lots of baby's breath.

Table setting   Use your pastel pink or blue linens. Wrap individual settings of silver in pink napkins and tie them with a blue bow. (This needn't be expensive; gift-wrap ribbon works just fine!) If you're using paper plates, stack pink and blue ones on the table in alternating colors.

Seat of honor   Tie together a bunch of pink and blue balloons and tape to wall or ceiling above chair. Twist pink and blue ribbon streamers from balloons to chair. Or, use clear balloons and fill with pastel confetti. You can make this decoration part of your gift by rolling up one-, five- or ten-dollar bills and inserting them into colored balloons before you blow them up.

Baby Quilt

Invitations   With pinking shears, cut a square of patterned gift wrap, small-print wallpaper or calico fabric. Attach the square to the front of a piece of folded notepaper.

Name tags   Cut more squares of construction paper, again with pinking shears. Use a variety of colors. You can choose one color ahead of time to determine the winner of a door prize.

Gift idea   If you think guests would enjoy it, arrange to have them help you make a baby quilt before the shower. Give them each a square of fabric to embroider or applique. Ask them to return the squares to you far enough ahead of time so that you can assemble the quilt as a special shower gift.

Or ask guests to bring their squares to the party so you can all complete the quilt during the shower, if you and your guests are expert enough and would enjoy it. The mother-to-be is sure to have fond memories of your old-fashioned quilting bee. And the quilt may well become a treasured heirloom.

You can take the idea one step further, particularly if there are many guests to share the cost: Sew accessories to match the quilt. Include a diaper stacker, crib bumper, sheet, pillows or pillowcases.

Table setting   Cut rectangles of different fabrics (using your pinking shears again) for placemats. Or, buy paper napkins and paper plates in a patchwork design.

Ideas for Any Theme

Corsage   Make a corsage for the mother-to-be from fancy baby socks, colorful ribbons and silk flowers.

Cake   Make a "cake" by rolling cloth or disposable diapers in a tight roll. Decorate the cake with sock or bootie "roses," rattles and other baby items. Roll other small gifts between the diapers if you wish. The new parents can take the cake home and put the components to use.

Baby bottles   Fill several decorated plastic baby bottles with jellybeans, candies, bath crystals or bath beads in pretty colors. Give these to the mother-to-be. She can offer the candies to visitors in the hospital, and enjoy the bath crystals in a relaxing bath at home. (See Activities section).

Balloons   Arrange balloons and other baby items together in an attractive basket or other large container. Place this arrangement on the floor near the guest of honor.

Chapter Three Serving the Food

The watchwords here are: "Keep it *simple.*" If you want to serve a full, sit-down meal (one that requires a knife), limit your guests to the number of people you can seat comfortably at your dining room table or at card tables. Guests don't enjoy balancing a plate and a cup of coffee on their laps (even with a tray). If there are rolls to be buttered or meat to be cut, *forget it*!

One way to get around the meal problem is not to serve a meal. Instead, set out a variety of simple hors d'oeuvres, open-face sandwiches, and individual desserts. Serving these easy finger foods will:

- Bring people to the table for snacking, thus encouraging conversation.
- Keep conversation flowing. When people snack throughout a party, you don't need to disrupt lively conversations to serve a meal.
- Permit guests to eat as much or as little as they wish.

Choosing recipes that can be prepared well ahead of time gets you out of the kitchen and in on the fun. Two major factors to consider when choosing your menu are the time of day the party is held and the number of people you are serving. The most popular times for showers are weekend noons, weekend afternoons and weekday evenings. Of these, only the weekend noon requires a full meal. For the other times, simply supply a variety of snacks and desserts.

Extremely large parties will probably mean a simpler meal. You may want to make a greater variety of dishes for a large party, but you won't have time to fuss with intricate foods such as dainty canapes. Save those for smaller groups.

Whether your party is large or small, you'll want to keep beverages simple. You can save considerable last-minute fussing by serving beverages that can be prepared in quantity, rather than mixed in individual glasses.

Hors d'Oeuvres and Snacks

Tasty appetizers and snacks are probably the all-time favorite party foods, and there's no reason why they shouldn't be enjoyed at showers. These foods are fine for a party on a weekend afternoon, as well as for an evening party.

It's easy to serve snacks more nutritious—and, tastier—than the chips and dips available at the grocery store. In fact, you can serve a well-balanced "meal" consisting entirely of "tidbits." A thoughtful host also will include low-calorie foods such as fresh vegetables for those guests who may be watching calories.

Crab Hors d'Oeuvres

8 ounces cream cheese
2 tablespoons cream or half-and-half
lemon juice

1 teaspoon Worcestershire sauce
cocktail sauce
1 small can crab meat, drained

Soften cream cheese. Thin with cream, lemon juice and Worcestershire sauce. Spread evenly on a plate. Spread a thin layer of cocktail sauce over cream cheese mixture; sprinkle crabmeat on top. Chill. Serve with knife and crackers and toast squares. Serves 10-20.

Blue Cheese Nuggets

4 ounces blue-veined cheese
1 tablespoon heavy cream
2 teaspoons brandy

2 tablespoons walnuts, coarsely ground
6 tablespoons wheat germ

Cream cheese, cream and brandy together. Stir in walnuts and chill. Line a cookie sheet with waxed paper. Pour wheat germ into a small saucer. Form cheese mixture into small, round balls, rolling about 1/2 teaspoon of the cheese mixture at a time between the palms of your hands. Roll each ball in the wheat germ and place on the cookie sheet. Refrigerate for at least 1 hour. (These also freeze well.) Serve with toothpicks. Makes 40 nuggets.

Open-Face Shrimp Sandwiches

4 1/2-ounce can deveined, broken shrimp, drained
3 scallions, both white and green parts, thinly sliced
3 tablespoons sour cream
4 tablespoons mayonnaise
6 tablespoons Parmesan cheese, finely grated
white pepper to taste
14 slices party rye bread
14 whole shrimp, cleaned and cooked
14 tiny sprigs of fresh parsley or mint

Drain shrimp. Combine scallions, sour cream, mayonnaise, Parmesan cheese and a dash of white pepper with shrimp. Mix by hand until almost smooth. Spread each slice of bread with 1 tablespoon shrimp mixture. Top each with a shrimp and a sprig of parsley or mint. Serve cold. Yields 14 open-face sandwiches.

Spinach Dip

10-ounce package chopped spinach
1 1/2 cups sour cream
1 cup mayonnaise
1 envelope vegetable soup mix
8-ounce can water chestnuts, drained and chopped
3 chopped green onions or 2 teaspoons minced onions
1 loaf sheepherder's bread or sourdough bread

Thaw spinach and squeeze out liquid. Add remaining ingredients and blend well. Cover; refrigerate at least 2 hours before serving. To serve, carve out center of bread; break into bite-size pieces and arrange on a tray around the loaf. Stir dip thoroughly and pour into hollowed-out loaf. Can also be served with crackers. Serves 10-20.

Salmon Ball

16-ounce can red salmon, with bones and skin removed, drained
8-ounce package cream cheese, softened
1 small onion, minced
2 tablespoons lemon juice
1/2 cup parsley, minced
1/4 cup nuts, chopped

Flake salmon into a bowl. Blend in cream cheese. Add onion and lemon juice. Mix well. Shape into a ball. Wrap in wax paper and chill until firm. Roll ball in parsley and chopped nuts before serving. Serves 10-20.

Quickies

cocktail rye or caraway rye bread
mayonnaise
onion, grated
Parmesan or Romano cheese, grated

Spread bread squares generously with mayonnaise. Top with grated onion and Parmesan or Romano cheese. Bake at 350° until browned.

Salmon Dip

16-ounce can salmon, with bones and
    skin removed, drained
8-ounce package cream cheese
1/2 teaspoon liquid smoke

1 tablespoon horseradish
2 tablespoons mayonnaise
1 to 2 tablespoons dry parsley
1 tablespoon lemon juice

Mix all ingredients together. Use as a dip with potato chips or spread on crackers or small rounds of cocktail rye. Serves 10-20.

Curried Egg and Artichoke Spread

6 eggs, hard-boiled, peeled
1 can artichoke hearts, drained
1/4 cup mayonnaise

1/2 cup sour cream
salt and pepper, to taste
1 teaspoon curry powder, or to taste

Chop hard-boiled eggs and artichoke hearts together. Add mayonnaise, sour cream, salt, pepper and curry powder to taste. Spread on crackers or small rounds of cocktail rye. Serves 10-20.

Marshmallow Fruit Dip

3 1/2 ounces marshmallow cream
1 tablespoon lemon juice
1 tablespoon orange juice

1/2 teaspoon orange or lemon peel,
    grated
1/4 cup salad dressing

Mix together and serve as a dip for fresh fruit. Serves 8-10.

Artichoke Squares

2 jars (6-ounce) marinated artichoke
    hearts
2 medium onions, chopped
1 clove garlic, crushed
4 eggs, beaten
1/2 cup bread crumbs
1/4 teaspoon salt
1/2 teaspoon pepper

1/2 teaspoon oregano
1/2 teaspoon Tabasco sauce
8 ounces sharp cheddar cheese,
    shredded
2 tablespoons parsley, chopped
Parmesan cheese, grated
paprika

Drain marinade from one jar of artichokes into skillet. Discard marinade in second jar. Chop artichokes and set aside. Sauté onions and garlic in marinade for 5 minutes. Combine beaten eggs, crumbs, seasonings, cheddar cheese and parsley with sauteed onions. Add artichokes. Pour into greased 8″ x 8″ pan. Bake at 325° for 30 minutes or until set. Sprinkle with Parmesan cheese and paprika during last 5 minutes of baking. Cut into squares and serve. Serves 8-10.

Crescent Rolls With Gouda

1 package of 8 refrigerator crescent rolls
1/2 pound gouda cheese

1 egg white, lightly beaten
sesame seeds

Lay the crescent roll dough out on a cookie sheet in a star pattern. Place gouda cheese in the middle and wrap the rolls around the cheese. Pinch the crescent rolls to plug any holes and brush the tops with egg white. Sprinkle sesame seeds over entire ball. Bake at 325° for 15-20 minutes or until golden brown. Slice into wedges to serve; serve warm. Serves 8-12.

Baked Mushrooms

8 mushroom caps, 1 1/2 inch or larger
    in diameter
1/3 cup butter or margarine

2 tablespoons sherry
1/4 teaspoon thyme
salt and pepper to taste

Rinse and dry mushrooms, removing stems from caps. Place mushrooms upside down in a shallow baking dish. Melt butter. Add sherry and thyme and bring to a boil. Spoon liquid into caps until full. Sprinkle with salt and pepper. Bake at 325° for 30-40 minutes, until tender. Serves 8.

Chinese Chicken Wings

1 cup water
1 cup soy sauce
1 cup brown or white sugar
1/4 cup pineapple juice

3/4 cup oil
1 teaspoon ginger
1 teaspoon garlic powder
20 to 24 chicken wings, cut in half

Mix all ingredients except chicken wings in a blender or food processor. Pour over chicken wings and marinate. When ready to bake wings, pour 1/2 cup of marinade in jelly roll pan, reserving remaining marinade for basting. Place wings on top of marinade. Bake at 350° for 45-60 minutes. Brush with reserved marinade. These freeze well. Serves 12-15.

Sugared Grapes

seedless red and/or green grapes
granulated sugar
egg whites

Wash grapes, separate into bunches of 3 to 6 grapes and set out on paper towels to dry. Beat egg whites. Dip grapes into egg whites, then roll in sugar. Set on waxed paper to dry. Refrigerate. These grapes are not only cool and refreshing, but are also extremely pretty. They can be used as a garnish for a plate of cold meats or other foods.

Other Ideas

- Wrap a slice of prosciutto around a kiwi fruit wedge or a melon wedge.
- Remove pimientos from stuffed green olives and substitute smoked almonds.
- Boil small new potatoes. Dry. Cut in half and scoop out the centers from each, leaving a 1/4 inch shell. Fill cavities with sour cream and top with a good sprinkling of red or black caviar.
- Fry bacon strips until crisp but pliable. Wrap around avocado slices brushed with lemon juice.
- Deviled eggs are good as both appetizer and garnish.

Luncheons and Brunches

These meals lend themselves well to a variety of foods. You can be as creative as you wish! Or, simply serve your favorite old stand-bys. Egg dishes, casseroles, sandwiches, fruit salads, poultry or seafood salads, and soups are all appropriate. Your favorite desserts may be welcome, too, especially if you provide a low-calorie option.

One easy approach is a salad potluck. You provide a variety of dressings. The guests bring different types of lettuce, spinach, tomatoes, and other salad ingredients. Make sure these are chopped well so they'll be easy to eat. Then simply arrange the ingredients on a buffet and let your guests create their own salads.

Remember that the foods people enjoy most at all kinds of parties are those that can be eaten easily. Don't make an exception for the food you serve at a shower. Most of your favorite party recipes are also appropriate for showers.

And don't hesitate to serve foods that are easy to prepare. Guests will enjoy the foods you serve, but they are not the reason for the party. Be as fancy as you wish, but feel free not to fuss. Simple foods are often the best.

Impossible Quiche

12 slices bacon, fried and crumbled
1 cup Swiss cheese, shredded
4 eggs
2 cups milk

1/3 cup onion
1/2 cup Bisquick
salt
pepper

Put bacon and cheese in bottom of greased 9-inch pie pan. Blend remaining ingredients for 1 minute; pour into pan. Bake at 350° for 50-55 minutes. Let stand 5 minutes before serving. Serves 6-8.

Elegant Eggs

6 tablespoons butter
1 medium onion, thinly sliced
12 ounces mushrooms, thinly sliced
2 cans (6-ounce) crab meat, drained
4 1/2-ounce can tiny shrimp, drained
8 eggs

1 cup sour cream
4 tablespoons dry sherry
1/8 teaspoon nutmeg
salt and pepper, freshly ground
paprika

Preheat oven to 350°. In large skillet, melt 4 tablespoons butter over low to medium heat. Saute onions and mushrooms until most of mushroom juice has evaporated. Remove from heat. Add remaining 2 tablespoons butter. When melted, stir in crab meat and shrimp and toss gently until shellfish are coated with butter. Let mixture cool completely.

In large mixing bowl, beat eggs well and add sour cream, sherry, nutmeg, salt and pepper; stir vigorously until mixed well. Pour egg mixture into skillet and stir to combine everything. Divide contents of skillet evenly between 2 greased, 9-inch pie plates. Sprinkle a little paprika over each pie.

Bake for 45-60 minutes, or until a toothpick inserted in center comes out clean. Let pies stand for 10 minutes, then cut into wedges and serve immediately.

If you want to make the eggs the day before your party, bake it and let the dish cool completely. At this point the eggs can be covered and stored in the refrigerator for a day. Before reheating, let the eggs come to room temperature for 30-45 minutes. Reheat in 350° oven for 20-30 minutes, until warmed through. Serves 8-10.

Cheese and Egg Brunch

6 slices bread, cubed
1 large can mushrooms, drained
1/2 cup stuffed olives, sliced
3/4 cup sharp cheddar cheese, grated
3/4 cup Swiss cheese, grated

4 eggs, beaten
2 cups milk
1/2 teaspoon dry mustard
1/2 teaspoon salt

Place half the bread crumbs in a 3-quart casserole. Layer with mushrooms, olives and cheese. Top with remaining bread crumbs. Combine beaten eggs, milk, mustard and salt. Pour over crumb mixture. Refrigerate overnight. Bake uncovered at 350° for 1 hour. Let stand 10 minutes before cutting. Serve with sausage, bacon and breads. Serves 8.

Eggs Lorraine

1 package Jimmy Dean sausage
  (original flavor)
2 tablespoons butter or margarine
2 cups cheddar cheese, grated

12 eggs, beaten
2/3 cup whipping cream
salt and pepper, to taste

Brown sausage; drain. Melt butter or margarine in a 9″ x 13″ pan. Sprinkle half the sausage on bottom of pan, then add half the cheese. Beat eggs with cream until frothy; pour over sausage and cheese in pan. Top with remaining sausage and cheese. Bake uncovered at 350° for 30 minutes. Serves 8-12.

Cream of Artichoke Soup

1 can (buffet-size) artichoke hearts,
  drained
1 can (10 1/2-ounce) cream of chicken
  soup
2 cups milk

1 cup cream
2 cups chicken broth
black pepper, freshly ground
1 to 2 bay leaves, if desired

Slice artichoke hearts crosswise. Mix all ingredients in saucepan; heat just to boiling. Remove bay leaves before serving. Serves 6. This recipe can be made ahead of time and refrigerated; reheat just before serving.

California Cream Soup

1 can (10 1/2-ounce) cream of celery
  soup
1 can (10 1/2-ounce) cream of chicken
  soup
2/3 cup light cream
2 cups milk

3/4 teaspoon salt
1/8 teaspoon pepper
3/4 cup avocado, chopped
1/4 cup ripe olives, sliced
1/4 cup pimiento, chopped

Mix soups, cream, milk, salt and pepper in large saucepan. Cook over low heat to simmer. Stir in remaining ingredients. Continue heating slowly for several minutes. Yields 7 1/2 cups of soup.

Zucchini Soup

1 medium onion, chopped
1/4 cup butter
4 cups chicken broth
12 cups zucchini, shredded
1/2 cup parsley, chopped

1/4 cup dill weed
1/4 cup basil
1 1/2 cup light cream or half cream and
    half buttermilk
salt and pepper to taste

Sauté onion in butter until golden. Add broth, zucchini and seasonings. Simmer about 25 minutes or until tender. Cool. Puree in food processor or blender. Add cream, salt and pepper. Chill at least 4 hours. Serves 12-14. Can be served hot.

Parsley-Lettuce Soup

1 pound potatoes
1 medium onion, coarsely chopped
1 clove garlic, finely chopped
2 teaspoons fresh or 1/2 teaspoon dried
    tarragon
salt and pepper to taste
3 cups chicken broth (or 2 cans chicken
    broth plus water to make 3 cups
    liquid)

1/2 cup dry white wine
1 cup plus 2 tablespoons fresh parsley,
    finely chopped
1/2 head romaine lettuce, finely
    chopped
4 ounces cream cheese, softened
1 cup heavy cream

Wash and peel potatoes and cut into chunks. In a medium saucepan, combine potatoes, onion, garlic, tarragon, salt, pepper, chicken broth and wine. Bring to a boil, then lower heat and cover. Simmer until potatoes are tender, about 15-20 minutes. Halfway through the cooking, add lettuce and 1 cup parsley.

In blender or food processor, puree potato mixture with cream cheese until smooth (blend in 2 or 3 batches).

To serve soup cold, add cream at this point. Refrigerate until chilled. May be covered and stored in refrigerator for 1-2 days.

To serve soup hot, refrigerate it without adding cream. Cover and store for 1-2 days. Shortly before serving, reheat soup over low to medium heat. Add cream and reheat again without letting soup boil. Sprinkle remaining 2 tablespoons of parsley over each portion as a garnish. Serves 10-20.

Hot or Cold Green Pea Soup

1 small onion, quartered
2 medium potatoes, peeled and cut into eighths
5 1/2 cups chicken broth
2 to 2 1/2 pounds fresh peas, shelled or 2 packages (10-ounce) frozen, tiny peas

1/2 teaspoon dried basil, crumbled
salt and white pepper, freshly ground to taste
1/4 cup dry vermouth
6 tablespoons sour cream

Place onion and potatoes in large saucepan and add 4 cups chicken broth. Bring to a boil. Then lower heat and simmer, covered, for 15 minutes or until potatoes are tender. Add peas, basil, salt and pepper to the broth. Simmer for another 5-7 minutes. In a food processor fitted with a steel blade, process mixture until smooth. (Blend in 2 batches.) Return pureed mixture to saucepan and add remaining chicken broth and vermouth. Stirring occasionally, reheat soup over low heat to let the flavors blend, about 15 minutes. Season to taste.

If serving cold, let soup cool completely and refrigerate until chilled.

At this point, soup can be stored in the refrigerator for 2-3 days. If serving hot, reheat over low to medium heat until soup is piping hot. Stir occasionally; do not let soup boil. Serve both cold and hot versions with a dollop of sour cream. Serves 6.

Broccoli Cheese Soup

2 tablespoons butter
1 medium onion, coarsely chopped
1 small clove garlic, halved
2 packages (10 ounces) frozen broccoli spears or chopped broccoli
salt and pepper to taste

1/4 teaspoon oregano
1/2 cup water
1/2 cup dry white wine
1/2 cup sharp cheddar cheese, grated
3 1/2 cups chicken broth
1/4 to 1/2 cup heavy cream

In large saucepan, melt butter over low to medium heat. Saute onion and garlic until tender; do not brown. Add broccoli, oregano, salt, pepper, water and wine. Bring to a boil over high heat, separating broccoli with a fork. Cover saucepan and reduce heat to simmer; cook until barely tender, about 5 minutes. Remove broccoli; cut into 2-inch pieces. Put broccoli, contents of saucepan, and cheese in a blender. Puree. Return puree to saucepan and stir in chicken broth. Reheat soup over low heat, stirring occasionally, about 15 minutes. Do not allow soup to boil.

At this point, soup can be held at room temperature for 3-5 hours, or cover and refrigerate for 2-3 days. Shortly before serving, reheat soup over low to medium heat. Stir in cream, taste for seasoning and reheat again without letting soup boil. Serve immediately. Serves 6.

Cream Cheese, Blue Cheese and Watercress Tea Sandwiches

1/2 bunch watercress
1 package (3-ounce) cream cheese, softened

2 ounces blue cheese
8 thin slices whole wheat bread

Wash and dry watercress, removing any tough stems. In small bowl, combine cheeses and stir to blend thoroughly. Cut crusts from bread and spread 4 slices with cheese mixture. Top cheese with 3 or 4 sprigs of watercress. Then top with remaining bread. Store in plastic wrap until just before serving. To serve, cut each sandwich into 4 triangles. Makes 16 small sandwiches.

Dill Cream Cheese Squares

4 ounces cream cheese, softened
2 tablespoons fresh dill, finely chopped
16 small sprigs of fresh dill

4 very thin slices of rye bread, cut in fourths or 16 small, party rye slices

Combine cream cheese with dill. Refrigerate overnight to enhance flavor. Let dill cream cheese come to room temperature and spread on rye squares. Garnish with dill sprigs.

Open-Face Tarragon Chicken Sandwiches

8 slices firm-textured white bread, crusts removed
1/2 cup tarragon butter

24 thin slices of chicken breast
parsley, minced

Toast bread slices on 1 side only, if you wish. Spread untoasted sides of bread with tarragon butter and arrange chicken slices on top. Sprinkle with parsley.

Tarragon Butter

1/4 pound unsalted butter
1 tablespoon dried tarragon, chopped, or
    2 tablespoons fresh tarragon

Place butter in small bowl and let soften. Cream butter by mashing against sides of bowl until light and fluffy. Add tarragon and blend well.

Open-Face Danish Sandwiches

dark pumpernickel bread in thin, square slices
rye bread in thin, square slices
unsalted butter
smoked salmon, sliced thin
sardines, with skin and bones removed

canned baby asparagus spears, drained
red onion, sliced thin
pepper, freshly ground
lemon, sliced thin
small sprigs of fresh dill

Spread bread slices with thin layer of butter. Cover some with smoked salmon, others with drained sardines. Garnish salmon sandwiches with small lengths of asparagus, lemon slices and fresh dill. Season sardine sandwiches with twists of pepper mill and garnish with slices of onion, lemon and sprigs of dill.

Prosciutto and Cream Cheese Squares

12 ounces cream cheese, softened
12 slices rye or pumpernickel bread

12 thin slices prosciutto
black olives

Spread cream cheese on bread slices. Top each with slice of prosciutto, folded. Slice several black olives. Crown each sandwich with a round of olive. Yields 12 sandwiches.

Egg Salad and Watercress Filling

3 eggs, hard-cooked and finely chopped
3 tablespoons watercress, chopped
1 teaspoon onion, minced

2 tablespoons mayonnaise
salt and cayenne to taste

Combine ingredients. Best when served chilled. Makes 1/2 cup.

Fantastic Chicken Salad

4 whole chicken breasts, boned
garlic powder
salt and pepper
2 tablespoons oil
2 tablespoons vinegar
2 tablespoons orange juice
1 head romaine lettuce, chopped
1 head iceberg lettuce, chopped
1 bunch spinach, torn
1 package (8-ounce) bean sprouts
4 ounces Swiss cheese, shredded

1/4 cup fresh dill, chopped
3 avocados, peeled and quartered
1 can (6-ounce) ripe olives, pitted and drained
1 can (8-ounce) sliced water chestnuts, drained
4 eggs, hard-cooked and quartered
1 jar (2 1/2-ounce) pimientos, sliced
1 red onion, sliced
fresh mushrooms, optional

Dressing:
1 pint mayonnaise
1/4 cup chili sauce
1/4 cup pickle relish
2 tablespoons onion, grated

Season chicken with garlic powder, salt and pepper. Bake at 350° until tender, about 30 minutes. Cut into large chunks. Marinate in oil, vinegar and orange juice for 24 hours in the refrigerator. When ready to serve, combine remaining salad ingredients with chicken and mix well. Combine dressing ingredients. Toss with salad. Serves 14.

Broccoli Salad

3 bunches raw broccoli (flowerets only)
1 cup vinegar
1 tablespoon sugar
1 tablespoon dill weed
1 teaspoon salt

1 teaspoon pepper
1 teaspoon garlic salt
1 1/2 cup vegetable oil
8 to 10 lettuce leaves

Put broccoli flowerets in a bowl. Mix remaining ingredients, except lettuce leaves and pour over broccoli. Blend well. Cover and refrigerate 24 hours. Drain and serve on lettuce leaves or as a relish. Serves 8-10.

Tropical Fruit Salad

1 can (20-ounce) pineapple chunks
1 can (11-ounce) mandarin oranges
1 can (8-ounce) green grapes, drained
1 to 2 bananas, peeled and sliced
1 avocado, peeled and sliced

1/2 cup sugar
1 tablespoon flour
1 egg, slightly beaten
1/4 cup lemon juice

Drain pineapple and oranges, save juices separately. Combine drained fruits with bananas and avocado. Prepare dressing by combining sugar, flour, egg, lemon juice and pineapple juice. If necessary, use reserved orange juice to make 3/4 cup liquid. Mix well. Cook slowly, stirring constantly until thickened. Cool; mix with salad fruits. Serve in lettuce-lined bowl. Serves 6-8.

7-Layer Lettuce Salad

1 head lettuce, torn
1/2 cup celery, diced
1/2 cup green pepper, diced
1/2 cup onion, diced
1 package frozen peas, cooked, cooled
    and drained

1 cup salad dressing
2 teaspoons sugar
6 ounces American cheese, shredded
6 slices bacon, fried

Arrange first 5 ingredients in a bowl. Spread salad dressing over the top; be sure it spreads to the edge of the bowl to seal. Sprinkle 2 teaspoons of sugar on salad dressing. Sprinkle cheese and crumble bacon on top. Cover tightly and refrigerate overnight. Toss and serve. Serves 10-12.

Honey Dressing

2/3 cup sugar
1 teaspoon dry mustard
1 teaspoon paprika
1 teaspoon celery seed
1/3 cup honey

5 tablespoons vinegar
1 tablespoon lemon juice
1 teaspoon onion, grated
1/4 teaspoon salt
1 cup salad oil

Mix all ingredients except oil in a blender. Gradually add oil. Drizzle over fresh fruit to serve. Makes one pint.

Fruit Salad In Melon Rings

1 can mandarin oranges, drained
1 can fruit cocktail, drained
1 can crushed pineapple, drained
1 jar maraschino cherries, chopped and
    drained
2 tablespoons strawberry or cherry Jell-O

1 cup colored miniature marshmallows
1/2 cup walnuts, chopped
1 cup (1/2 pint) whipped cream
1 tablespoon mayonnaise
3 to 4 melons—cantaloupe, honeydew
    or both

Combine all ingredients except melons. Chill until firm. Wash melons. Slice ends of melons to expose seeds; scoop out seeds and membrane. Cut melons crosswise to form rings approximately 1-inch thick. Fill with scoops of fruit salad. Serves 15-20.

Chicken, Rice and Walnut Casserole

2 tablespoons butter
2 onions, minced
8 cups brown rice, cooked
1 1/2 cups sharp cheddar cheese,
    grated
1/2 cup Parmesan cheese, freshly
    grated
4 large eggs, lightly beaten
1 cup chicken broth

2 garlic cloves, minced
1 teaspoon dried sage
1/2 teaspoon cayenne
pinch of salt and pepper
1/2 cup walnuts, chopped
1 cup fresh parsley, chopped
3 cups cooked chicken, cut in bite-size
    pieces

Melt butter in small skillet. Saute onion until translucent. Combine onion with remaining ingredients except walnuts and 1/4 cup of cheddar cheese. Transfer to lightly oiled 2-quart baking dish. Top with walnuts and reserved cheese. Bake at 350° for 30-40 minutes or until top is golden. Serves 8-10.

Desserts

When you're entertaining in the afternoon or evening, you can offer just a dessert and coffee if you wish. Consider your guests when you choose between a "sinfully rich" triple chocolate whipped cream bar and a simple, fresh fruit plate. If you don't know the preferences of your guests, offer a choice. Include at least one alternative not made with chocolate, since many pregnant and nursing women avoid chocolate.

Silver White Cake

For 2 9-inch layers:
2 2/3 cups flour, sifted
1 7/8 cups sugar
4 1/2 teaspoons baking powder
1 teaspoon salt
2/3 cup soft shortening
1 1/4 cups milk
2 teaspoons flavoring
5 egg whites

For 2 8-inch layers:
2 1/8 cups flour
1 1/2 cups sugar
3 1/2 teaspoons baking powder
3/4 teaspoon salt
1/2 cup soft shortening
1 cup milk
1 1/2 teaspoons flavoring
4 egg whites

Sift flour, sugar, baking powder and salt together. Add shortening. Pour a little more than half the milk over mixture and add flavoring. Beat 2 minutes. Add remaining milk and egg whites. Beat 2 more minutes. Generously grease and flour cake pans. Pour mixture into prepared pans. Bake at 350° for 30-35 minutes or until cake tests done. Cool. Finish with desired filling and frosting. Elegant with almond cream filling and a delicious frosting such as the one below.

Silver White Icing

1 cup shortening (not butter)
2 tablespoons butter
1/4 cup flour
2 tablespoons milk
2 egg whites

1 teaspoon salt
4 cups powdered sugar
4 teaspoons flavoring (almond is very good)

Place all ingredients in large mixing bowl and beat on high speed for 10 minutes. This frosting is very stiff; very good for decorating.

Frozen Lemon Delight

3 eggs, separated
1/2 cup sugar
juice of one lemon

1/2 pint whipping cream
24-30 vanilla wafers
15-20 cupcake papers

Beat egg yolks, sugar and lemon juice just until thick. Whip cream and fold into egg mixture. Beat egg whites until stiff and fold. Crush vanilla wafers and put three-fourths of the crumbs on bottom of cupcake papers. Add lemon mixture. Sprinkle remaining crumbs on top. Freeze. Remove from freezer and place in refrigerator about 10 minutes before serving. Makes 15-20 servings.

Chocolate Peanut Butter Bars

2 1/2 cups powdered sugar
2 cups graham cracker crumbs
1 cup peanut butter

1 cup margarine, melted
12-ounce package chocolate chips

Mix sugar and crumbs together with peanut butter. Add melted margarine and mix. Pat firmly in 9" x 13" pan. Melt chocolate chips and spread on top. Refrigerate until firm. Cut into bars. Makes 100 1-inch square bars.
Variation: Peanut butter mixture can be rolled into balls and dipped in the melted chocolate.

German Chocolate Bars

1 bag (14-ounce) caramels
1 cup evaporated milk
1 package German chocolate cake mix

3/4 cup butter
1 cup chocolate chips
1 cup nuts

Combine caramels with 2/3 cup milk. Melt in double boiler over low heat or in microwave. In separate bowl, mix cake mix, butter and remaining 1/3 cup milk. Press half this mixture into ungreased 9" x 13" pan. Bake at 350° for 6 minutes. Remove from oven. Sprinkle with chocolate chips and nuts. Pour melted caramel mixture over nuts and chips. Top with remaining cake mixture. Bake 20 minutes longer. Cool completely before cutting. Keep refrigerated. Makes 50-75.

Impossible Cheesecake

3/4 cup milk
2 teaspoons almond flavoring
2 eggs
1 cup sugar

1/2 cup Bisquick baking mix
2 packages (8 ounces each) cream
    cheese, softened
Slivered almonds

Preheat oven to 350°. Blend milk, vanilla, eggs, sugar and baking mix in blender on high for 15 seconds. Cut cream cheese into 1/2-inch cubes. Add cream cheese to mixture. Blend on high for 2 minutes. Pour into greased 9-inch pie plate or muffin tin lined with foil cupcake papers. Bake until center is set, about 40-45 minutes. Cool. Top with slivered almonds.

Sunshine Orange Cake

1 package yellow cake mix
1/2 cup oil
4 eggs

1 can (11-ounce) mandarin oranges
    with juice

Mix all ingredients. Beat 2 minutes. Bake at 350° for 30-40 minutes. Serves 18-25.

Frosting:
8 ounces Cool Whip
1 small box instant vanilla pudding

1 can (8-ounce) crushed pineapple with
    juice

Mix together and spread on cooled cake. Keep refrigerated.

Bourbon-Soaked Chocolate Truffles

7 ounces semisweet baking chocolate
1 ounce unsweetened baking chocolate
4 tablespoons bourbon, whiskey or dark
    Jamaica rum
1 stick (4 ounces) unsalted butter, cut
    into 1-inch pieces

2 tablespoons strong liquid coffee
6 ounces ginger snaps
1/2 cup unsweetened cocoa powder
1/4 cup powdered coffee
paper or foil candy cups

Break chocolate into small pieces; place in top half of double boiler with bourbon or rum and liquid coffee. Cover, place over boiling water, and turn off heat under it. When chocolate is melted and smooth (in 5 minutes or so), beat in butter with electric mixer. Pulverize gingersnaps in a blender and add to chocolate mixture. Beat thoroughly. Chill for several hours.

Mix the cocoa powder with the powdered coffee and spread on a plate. With a soup spoon or teaspoon, depending on the size you wish, dig out gobs of the chocolate mixture and form into rough, round shapes. Roll in the cocoa/coffee powder mixture and place in candy or cookie cups. Refrigerate in a covered container until serving time. Truffles may be refrigerated for several weeks or frozen. Makes 20 to 40 pieces, depending on the size. These are very rich, so you may want them small.

Iced Almonds

2 cups whole blanched almonds
1 cup sugar
4 tablespoons butter or margarine

1 teaspoon vanilla
salt

Heat almonds, sugar and butter in heavy skillet over medium heat. Stir constantly until almonds are toasted and sugar is golden brown—about 15 minutes. Stir in vanilla. Spread nuts on a foil-covered cookie sheet. Sprinkle with salt. Cool, then break into chunks.

Phyllis's Raspberry Dessert

1 box vanilla wafers
1/2 cup butter
2 cups powdered sugar
2 eggs
1 cup chopped nuts

1 package raspberry Jell-O
1 cup boiling water
2 packages frozen raspberries
2 cups whipping cream

Crush vanilla wafers. Sprinkle half the wafers in the bottom of a 9″ x 13″ pan. Soften butter and cream together with powdered sugar. Add eggs one at a time. Spread mixture over crumbs. Sprinkle chopped nuts on top. Dissolve Jell-O in water. Add frozen raspberries. Stir until melted. Cool. When thick, spread over mixture. Whip the cream and spread over Jell-O layer. Add remaining crumbs and refrigerate. Serves 18-25.

Turtles

pecans
1 1/2 packages caramels

Frosting:
1 square sweet chocolate
1 tablespoon butter
1/2 teaspoon vanilla

1 cup powdered sugar
2 tablespoons hot milk

Cluster pecans in threes on greased cookie sheet. Put a caramel on each cluster of pecans. Warm in oven at 325° until caramel softens—4-8 minutes. Flatten with buttered spatula or spoon. Cool slightly, but frost while still warm. This gives frosting a glazed look.

For frosting, melt chocolate and butter. Add vanilla, powdered sugar and hot milk. Add extra sugar for more body. Beat with a spoon until smooth.

Blueberry Sour Cream Torte

Crust:
3/4 cup butter, softened
1/4 cup sugar
2 egg yolks

2 cups flour
1 teaspoon baking powder
1/2 teaspoon salt

Filling:
4 cups fresh blueberries
3/4 cup sugar
1/4 cup quick-cooking tapioca

1/2 teaspoon lemon rind, grated
1/2 teaspoon cinnamon
1/8 teaspoon nutmeg

Topping:
2 egg yolks, slightly beaten
2 cups sour cream

1/2 cup sugar
1 teaspoon vanilla

For crust, cream butter and sugar. Add egg yolks and beat until fluffy. Combine flour, baking powder and salt. Blend into creamed mixture. Press 2/3 of mixture in a 9-inch springform pan. Bake at 400° for 10 minutes. Cool. Reduce oven temperature to 350°. Press remaining crust mixture 1 1/2 inches up side of pan.

For filling, combine blueberries, sugar, tapioca, lemon rind, and spices in saucepan. Let stand 15 minutes. Cook and stir until bubbly. Pour into crust.

For topping, blend egg yolks, sour cream, sugar and vanilla. Spoon over fruit filling. Bake at 350° for 45 minutes. Cool and refrigerate until chilled. Serves 12.

Low-Calorie Dessert Ideas

Cheese and Fruit   A simple, nutritious alternative to rich desserts is a large round of dessert or soft cheese, such as Camembert or Brie, placed in the center of a large platter and surrounded by slices of crusty French bread, tasty crackers, and slices of fresh fruit. (Apples work particularly well with this idea and are usually available all year 'round.)

Watermelon Basket   An attractive way to serve fresh fruit is to carve out a whole watermelon in the shape of a basket. Start by placing the watermelon on the table, testing it to find which side it rests on most sturdily. Before cutting, use a pencil to trace the outline of the handle (make sure it is thick enough so that it won't wilt) and the basket. The basket sides can be straight, jagged or fluted, depending on your imagination and skill with a kitchen knife. Be sure to leave a large enough "basket" to fill with fresh fruit including melon balls, seedless grapes, pineapple chunks, kiwi fruit slices, halved strawberries—whatever fresh fruit is in season. (Note: it's a good idea to de-pit cherries and other fruits before putting them in the basket.) You can also decorate the exterior of the basket with cherries, strawberries, pineapple, and other fruit on toothpicks.

Date 'N Nut Bars
2 cups chopped, pitted dates
1 cup chopped walnuts
1 cup whole wheat flour
1/4 cup corn oil
1 tablespoon vanilla extract

1/4 teaspoon salt
2 eggs, lightly beaten
1 16-ounce can of unsweetened, crushed
   pineapple, drained.

Combine the dates, walnuts and flour, mixing well. In another bowl, combine the remaining ingredients and mix well. Combine the two mixtures in a large bowl and mix thoroughly. Spoon the dough into a non-stick baking dish. Bake in a preheated oven (350°) for 30-35 minutes. Cool and cut into 36 bars.

Flavored Melon Balls

1/4 cup unsweetened frozen apple juice concentrate, thawed

1/2 teaspoon ground anise seed
4 cups of assorted melon balls

Combine ingredients, mixing well. Refrigerate until cold before serving.

Pumpkin Pudding

1 16-ounce carton ricotta cheese
2 cups mashed cooked pumpkin (or canned pumpkin)
3 tablespoons fructose

1 tablespoon ground cinnamon
1 teaspoon allspice
1/8 teaspoon mace
1-1/2 tablespoons vanilla extract

Blend all ingredients in food processor (with metal blade) until mixture is smooth. Refrigerate until cold, then serve half cup of pudding in sherbert dishes. Top with low-cal whipped cream. (See recipe in this section.)

Carob Mousse

1/2 cup carob powder, sifted
1/2 cup hot water
1 1/2 teaspoons instant decaffeinated coffee
3 large eggs, separated
1/4 teaspoon cream of tartar

2 tablespoons sugar
1/2 teaspoon vanilla
3 tablespoons sugar
1/2 cup Low-Calorie Whipped Cream (recipe below)

Topping:
1/4 cup blanched almond slivers
1/2 cup Low-Calorie Whipped Cream (recipe below)

Put carob in saucepan and slowly add hot water. Stir constantly until smooth. Bring to boil. Add coffee and boil 2 minutes. Remove from heat. Cool 10 minutes. Beat in egg yolks, 2 tablespoons sugar and vanilla until mixture thickens. Blend in carob mix. Beat egg whites and cream of tartar until soft peaks form. Slowly add 3 tablespoons sugar and beat to stiff peaks. Fold whites and cream into the carob mix. Chill for 2 hours. Top with almonds and a dollop of whipped cream. Serves 8-10.

Whipped Cream

1 cup evaporated skim milk
1 packet unflavored gelatin
1 teaspoon fresh lemon juice

Dissolve gelatin in milk. Freeze mixture in mixing bowl until ice crystals begin to form. With chilled beaters, whip milk at high speed until it triples in volume, adding lemon juice at the end of whipping.

Other Dessert Ideas

Place a paper doily on any non-iced cake. Sift powdered sugar over the doily. Lift doily gently off cake. Ring cake with fresh flowers and serve.

An elegant finishing touch for a plain white cake is to drizzle melted chocolate over white icing.

Beverages

Because pregnant women (and others) should steer clear of alcohol and caffeine, it makes sense to serve beverages other than alcoholic punches and coffee.

When you are deciding whether or not to serve alcohol at your shower, consider the attitudes of the expectant mother, other guests and yourself. Opinions may vary widely. Ask if she'd be more comfotable drinking juice as other guests drink wine, or whether it's best to eliminate liquor altogether.

Serving decaffeinated coffee is probably a good idea—it's easier than serving both kinds and more likely to make a hit with all of your guests than serving strictly the caffeinated variety.

Syrupy punches, long the staple of the "hen party," aren't the only option. Light, fruity punches are usually enjoyed by almost everyone.

June Punch

4 cups sugar
4 cups water
2 cups strong black tea
6 cans (6-ounce) frozen lemonade
2 cans (6-ounce) frozen orange juice

2 cans (No. 2) pineapple juice (5 cups)
2 cups fresh strawberries or 16-ounce
   package frozen strawberries
1 gallon water
2 quarts dry ginger ale

Make syrup by boiling sugar and 4 cups water for 10 minutes. Add tea and fruit juice concentrates. Chill 2-3 hours. Thaw frozen strawberries or cut up fresh strawberries. Reserve juice. Add strawberries, juice, water and ginger ale to punch. Pour over ice cubes or block of ice in punch bowl. Yields 60-70 servings.

Raspberry Punch

frozen concentrated raspberry juice
7-Up or Ginger Ale
frozen raspberries

Mix juice concentrate with water according to directions on the can. Add equal amounts of 7-Up or ginger ale and mix. Float frozen raspberries in punch.

Firecracker Punch

4 cups cranberry juice
1 1/2 cups sugar
4 cups pineapple juice

1 tablespoon almond extract
2 quarts ginger ale

Combine first 4 ingredients. Add ginger ale just before serving. Serves 30.

Apple Cider Punch

1 quart apple cider
2 cups cranberry juice
1 cup orange juice

1 can (12-ounce) apricot nectar
1 cup sugar
2 sticks cinnamon

Combine in sauce pan and simmer for 20 minutes. Garnish with orange slices decorated with cloves. Serves 20-25.

Southern Comfort Punch

1 fifth Southern Comfort or catawba
   juice
6-ounce can frozen orange juice

6-ounce can frozen lemonade
4-5 ounces lemon juice
3 quarts BubbleUp

Mix together and top with orange and lemon slices.

Orange Blossom Punch

1 jar (4-ounce) maraschino cherries,
   drained
1 can (8-ounce) pineapple chunks,
   drained

24 ounces champagne
1/2 gallon orange juice

Fill a 6-cup ring mold with water or juice. Drop in cherries and pineapple. Freeze. Pour champagne and orange juice in punch bowl. Unmold ice ring by dipping in 2 inches of hot water. Slide ring into punch.

Brandy Slush

2 cups sugar
9 cups water
2 cups brandy

1 can (12-ounce) frozen orange juice
1 can (12-ounce) frozen lemonade

Mix all ingredients together and freeze at least 24 hours. Put dollop of slush in each glass, then fill with 7-Up.

Mimosa Punch

Mix 1 part champagne with 2 parts orange juice.

Fruited Champagne Punch

2 large fresh peaches
1 pint fresh strawberries
1/2 cup sugar
1 bottle (3 1/4 cups or 750 ml.) Moselle
   wine

1 bottle (3 1/4 cups or 750 ml.) Rhine
   wine, chilled
1 bottle (3 1/4 cups or 750 ml.)
   champagne, chilled

Peel and slice peaches; wash and hull strawberries. Place peaches and strawberries in large punch bowl. Prick fruit with fork in several places so it will absorb wine. Sprinkle with sugar. Pour Moselle wine over fruit. Let stand at room tem-

perature for 2 hours. Just before serving. pour chilled Rhine wine and champagne over fruit. Add an ice ring. if you wish. Makes 3 quarts.
Variation: Replace the 3 bottles of wine with 3 bottles of sparkling catawba for a delicious alcohol-free punch.

Summer Sangria

1 cup sugar
1 1/2 cups water
1 cup orange juice
1/2 cup brandy
1 large orange, sliced and quartered

1 lime, sliced
1 cup honeydew melon balls
1 bottle (3 1/4 cups or 750 ml.) dry red
    or white wine, chilled, or
    catawba juice

Combine sugar and water in large pitcher: stir until sugar dissolves. Add orange juice, brandy, orange. lime and honeydew. Let stand 2 hours. Add ice cubes and stir in chilled wine just before serving. Makes 2 quarts.
Note: Vary fruit according to what is available and looks most colorful. Strawberries add contrast if using white wine.

Serving Suggestions

- When serving large trays of small items on your buffet table, prepare two complete trays of each item. Then, as the first tray on the table becomes depleted, the second complete tray can be brought out from the kitchen to replace it.
- Before pouring hot coffee or cold punch into a serving container, temper it with hot or cold water. Not only will it lessen the chance of breaking a glass pitcher, your beverages will stay hot (or cold) much longer.
- A basket with a handle makes a convenient and pretty hors d'oeuvres tray to pass from guest to guest. For an extra touch, tie a pastel ribbon on the handle and line it with a ruffled cloth.
- Soups can be as plain or as fancy as you wish; they need not be difficult to serve. Place a tureen on your table with a ladle and mugs or pretty paper "hot cups." Set out a bowl of croutons for garnish.

Special equipment

You might want to rent or borrow some of the following if you're planning a large affair:

Card tables and folding chairs	Large serving trays
Coffeemaker	Pitchers
Punch bowl and cups	Champagne glasses

Garnishes

A pretty garnish can add a festive touch to any serving tray or punch bowl. Here are a few ideas:

- Float an ice ring in a punch bowl or set it on a platter to keep appetizers cold. To make an ice ring, layer fruits such as cherries or citrus slices and water (or some of your punch) an inch at a time in a ring mold. Freeze each layer before adding the next. By using punch instead of water, you avoid diluting your punch as the ice melts.
- Traditional garnishes are carrot curls, sculpted lemons, radish flowers, tomato roses, and scallion brushes. Try them if you have time!
- Arrange a circle of shiny green lemon leaves around the edge of an hors d'oeuvres platter. Tuck in a few tiny mums and daisies and several small bunches of green grapes here and there.

Other eye-appealing garnishes:

- bright red cherry tomatoes
- bunches of watercress
- shiny olives
- pimiento strips
- avocado slices
- lemon, lime or orange slices
- hard-boiled egg slices
- cucumber slices
- baby dill pickles
- a sprinkling of paprika
- crisp parsley or mint sprigs
- crumbled cooked egg yolk

Keeping the Party Rolling

Chapter Four

Your guests are arriving this afternoon at three, and suddenly you wonder: What will we *do*? Should you plan an activity (shades of those stodgy old showers) or, leave guests free to entertain themselves?

If your guests are all acquainted with each other, there's no need to panic. Good friends, or another closely knit group, often like nothing more than a chance to relax and visit. Simply plan the same sorts of things you'd normally do together.

But if your group is comprised of strangers, or (even worse!) small groups who know each other and a few people who don't know anyone else, you may need to plan a few activies to create the relaxed, friendly ambiance you want. No one should feel left out of the fun. Many of the activities we've included here are excellent "icebreakers" that help to get conversation started so everyone can have a good time.

Don't confuse these activities with the "icebreakers" you remember from past baby showers. For some reason, the tradition of playing silly, sometimes embarrassing games has persisted. Such games have been the nemesis of baby showers for a number of years. Luckily, we don't have to continue the practice.

Instead, we've suggested activities that foster (rather than kill) spontaneous talk. You can lay out some of these games on a table, even the same table as the food, if there's room. Let people try them at their own pace. As they gather, their conversation will pick up naturally. And those who don't want to participate won't feel pressured.

Here are the major questions to ask when you consider whether an activity is appropriate:

1. Will the activity bring conversation to a screeching halt, without providing another type of entertainment?
2. Will it embarrass anyone or make them feel bad?
3. Will it foster pressure or competitiveness, creating hard feelings for those who don't win?

The Party is the Gift

In a sense, giving a baby shower is a gift in itself. The new mother (or both parents) is sure to feel special, and supported by the friendship of the group. The warm memories and good feelings you give the new parents are as meaningful as any more tangible gift they receive.

You can combine this gift of the shower itself with the gift of some tangible object, by creating something—at the shower. Working together on a project, such as tying a baby quilt, can be a relaxing shower activity. And the completed project will be both useful and a pleasant reminder of the day.

Many of the activities below result in a useful present. These activities produce a homemade parenting book, a keepsake book for the new baby, a photo album, hand-embroidered diapers, and a photo documentary of the shower. There are many other possibilities, of course. Just use your imagination—and your group's special talents and interests.

Best Wishes   Furnish a handmade or purchased guest book or poster and set it on the table with the name tags. (Some stores have specially designed posters for this purpose.) Put a sign near it requesting guests to sign their names and write a good wish and/or piece of advice for the baby as he or she grows. (For example, "May you grow healthy, happy and strong.")

"How My Baby Changed My Life"   Instruct your guests to bring a written story relating their own parenting experiences (of frustration, joy or humor) to the party. Then collect the stories in a homemade book for the new parents. You may want to furnish the paper to your

guests ahead of time if you want to use a certain type. Or, simply ask guests to use a uniform size of paper. Prepare a cover in advance; use decorated construction paper, a colored portfolio or a three-ring binder. Ask guests to read their stories at the party. (It's a good idea to warn them about this ahead of time!) Then clip or fasten their pages together in the book.

The Baby Profile

Have your guests help you "predict" the expected baby's attributes, without knowing they're doing it.

As each guest arrives, ask him or her to name an item in a category so that you can fill out the baby profile form (see the Appendix). The first guest should choose a sex, the second a first name, the third a last name and so on. To fill in the hair color and eye color blanks, ask someone to name any color. For the height blank, limit the possibilities to numbers between 54 and 84. Limit the weight answers to numbers between 95 and 300. Complete the occupation and hobby blanks. Add more categories, if necessary, so that each guest can answer a question.

Now the new baby's profile is complete. Your guests—and the new parents—will enjoy hearing that the baby will become "a female plumber, who has green hair and orange eyes, is over six feet tall, weighs 95 pounds, and eats chopped liver." You may want to give the new parents a copy of the profile for their baby book.

Lights, Camera, Action

Create a treasured memento by having someone record the shower on videotape or movie film. In years to come, "baby" may delight in seeing films of how his or her arrival into the world was happily anticipated by parents, family, and friends.

Instant Replay

If you have an instant camera, take pictures of the shower. Include shots of the buffet or dinner table before eating, one of each guest and several of the guests of honor as they open their gifts. Insert the photos in a photo album and give it to the new parents. The album will interest guests at the end of the shower and will serve later as a memento of the shower for the parents. Don't worry if you've left plenty of blank pages in the album; that way the parents can add their own photos of the baby's first year.

"Write Your Own Caption"

Make copies of the cartoons in the Appendix about the joys and frustrations of parenting. Then post them (along with pens and pencils) at the party. Display the cartoons together, or scattered here and there (at the name tag table, the coat room, the food table). Invite guests to write their own captions. Guests will enjoy reading each other's answers throughout the party. You can compile them and present them to the new parents at the end of the party.

Advice

To make introductions more interesting, have each guest relate his or her favorite piece of parenting advice. The advice could be either serious or funny. Someone in the group should record this sage wisdom, along with the names of the advisers, in a notebook for the new parents to keep. Or, make a tape recording of the advice session. This activity is fun even if the guests all know each other—just eliminate the introductions. And, of course, don't pressure anyone to join in. Some guests will be more eager to give advice than others!

Quilting Bee

What shower gift could be more welcome than a personalized baby quilt? You and your guests can create one in several ways. One way is to instruct guests to bring quilt squares to be joined together at the party (see Baby Quilt theme, page 21). Another is to have guests sign the back of a quilt with indelible marker. You can use a ready-made quilt or make a quilt yourself ahead of time. If you wish, you can embroider the signatures later.

Embroidery Party

If the new parents plan to use cloth diapers, you can give them a dozen (or more) and personalize them. Distribute a diaper to each guest at the shower, and provide embroidery needles and thread. Each guest can stitch a quick design of flowers, hearts, a rainbow—whatever—on a corner or the "seat" of the diaper. The new baby will have "hand-crafted" diapers and the new parents will have a special reminder of the shower and of each friend attending. Nobody needs to be an expert needleworker to join the fun. This activity is great for boosting conversation while everybody works together.

The Family Tree

On a large piece of paper, draw a large outline of a tree. Then ask guests to predict the characteristics of the new baby, based on traits of other members of the family (such as Grandpa's nose, Aunt Bernice's sense of humor, or, Daddy's broad shoulders and long legs). Record the predictions in spaces on the tree (along with the name of the predictor, if it is one person). Then present the finished tree to the mother-to-be to insert in baby's record book.

Getting Men Involved

With all the changes in childbirth over the last ten years, it's remarkable that so many people (particularly men) still consider showers to be "hen parties." But that's changing. Many men now know that a shower is a fun part of all the commotion surrounding a baby's birth. If the men you know agree, they might enjoy a "couples shower." If you're in doubt, make sure the men you invite understand what sort of party you're planning. You may have to dispel their stereotypes of a trite shower with "dainty" food and "dumb" games.

The key to planning a shower for men and women is to plan it as if it were any other kind of party they would enjoy. As with any party, a couples shower will be most relaxed if the male guests know each other well and especially if they know the father-to-be well. Gag gifts, "fatherly" advice (if the other men have children) and the company of friends combine to make such a shower an occasion to remember.

Listed here are some activities specifically geared toward men, though they can participate in others suggested in this chapter.

Roast   Ask guests to take turns telling their own stories about the baby's parents, applying them to the way the baby will be. Encourage humorous, outrageous—but friendly—recollections. The longer the guests have known the parents the funnier this activity will be.

Baby Pool   This is especially fun if your group enjoys betting at other times. Copy the baby pool form in the Appendix. Hand copies of the form out to guests. Then have guests estimate the unborn baby's date and time of birth, sex, length and weight.

Everyone will try harder if you offer a prize, so announce it now. You may want to take a collection for a savings account for the newborn: Collect 50 cents or a dollar per entry and allow guests to enter as many times as they wish.

Your guests will have to wait until after the baby is born to find out who wins this bet. To score, award 3 points for each "win"; 2 points for a second place; 1 point for a third; 2 points for the sex question. The person with the most points wins the baby pool. Be sure to award a prize.

Baby Trivia   Use the list of questions provided in the Appendix to play a version of baby shower trivia. You can play this game in at least two ways: Divide the group into teams and take turns asking questions; or, ask questions of the group at large. The first person to answer a question correctly gets a point. Or, make up your own rules. Add more questions to the list if you wish.

Other Fun Activities

You may want to focus on one of the following activities—or, try several. None should bog your party down with pressure or freeze it in silence. They're intended, instead, to get you laughing and talking. Try them and see.

Name Tags and Introductions   The first activity at your party may be to distribute name tags, if guests do not know each other. Set the blank tags out on a table so that your guests can add their own names as they arrive. The process may get them talking to each other. If not, when all the guests are seated, have them take turns introducing themselves and explaining briefly how each knows the expectant parents.

Name the Baby Food   Select ten or twelve jars of baby food and remove the labels. Mark each jar with a number. Set the jars out on a table and have guests guess the contents. (Provide paper and pencils.) Give a prize to the person who correctly identifies the greatest number and perhaps a prize to the person who comes up with the most creative names!

Guess the Name Tags   This is a new twist on an old game. Prepare the name tags in advance. Add a small picture of a baby-related item to each tag. (Trace or photocopy one of the designs in the Appendix, draw free-hand, or buy appropriate stickers.) As the guests arrive, attach their tag to their back. (Remember to put your mirrors away!) The guests then must ask each other questions about the item on their tag (only "yes" or "no" answers are permitted) until they guess the correct picture. This activity helps guests who don't know each other learn each other's names. The first (and maybe the last) person to guess his or her own picture could win a prize.

Who's the Baby?

Ask each of the guests to bring a baby picture of himself or herself. As guests arrive with their photos, keep them together somewhere out of the way until all of the photos are in. This way, the earlier guests don't have an "edge" on later arrivals. Provide a copy of the guest list for each guest, with a blank after each name on the list. Display the photos in a snapshot album with an identification number by each. Guests then fill out their forms, guessing which picture goes with which guest. The guest with the most correct guesses wins a prize. At the end of the party, when people have removed their photos, you can present the album to the guests of honor.

Guess the Beans

Put pink and blue jelly beans or other small candies in a fancy plastic baby bottle. (You can buy some bottles that are hand-painted, others that are molded into fun shapes—just be sure the bottle is transparent.)

Set this out on a table (maybe next to the name tags to help get things going right away). Also set out slips of paper with blanks for name and number guessed. After each guest has had a chance to guess the number of beans in the bottle, have them drop their entries into a box or bowl. Then read the entries and announce the winner. If you have a younger guest at the party, he or she may enjoy counting the beans just after the entries are submitted. Otherwise you may want to count them in advance.

This Is Your Life

It can be great fun to pattern your shower on this old TV show, especially if your guests are family members or old friends.

First, prepare a short slide show of the new parents when they were young. Or, show family movies, if they're available. Suggest that guests try to predict the attributes of the baby while watching the parents-to-be in action.

Next, include a "mystery guest," if you can. Choose someone who knew one of the expectant parents in the distant past. Keep the mystery guest (or guests) hidden while he or she shares some stories about that person. Then ask the new parents to guess who is talking about them. This is especially fun if you can include an unexpected—and welcome—acquaintance as your "mystery guest."

"Sure-Fire" Sex Determination

The following tests are much more fun than scientific; they are based on folklore and common "wisdom" for predicting an unborn baby's sex. Use the form in the Appendix to record your predictions. Then copy the form and give it to the expectant parents to put in the baby's book. After the baby is born, you can decide which predictions were most "accurate"!

1. Tie a silver needle or a gold ring to a piece of thread. Hold it over the unborn baby. If it spins, the baby is a girl. If it swings, the baby is a boy.
2. Lots of morning sickness? Then it's a boy.
3. How many cowlicks does the older sibling have? If the sibling has one cowlick, the baby will be the same sex as the sibling. If the older child has two or more, the baby will be the opposite sex.
4. If the baby is very active and kicks a lot, it's a boy.
5. If the mother's stomach appears small for her stage of pregnancy, it's a girl. If large, it's a boy.
6. If the mother is carrying the baby low, it's a boy; if high, it's a girl.
7. If the mother's face is tight and drawn, it's a boy. If her face has a soft, relaxed glow, it's a girl.
8. If the mother gained lots of weight early in the pregnancy, it's a girl.
9. If her right eye and breast are enlarged, it's a boy.
10. Ask the mother to hold her head still and look to the right and to the left. Watch her eyes. If there is a red line from the iris to the outside corner of her left eye, the baby is a girl. If there's one on the right eye, it's a boy.
11. If the mother is sick during her first trimester, the baby will be a girl. If her husband is sick during this time, it's a boy.

Baby's Fortune

Have each guest write a personality trait, physical trait or a "piece of luck" on a small piece of paper. Fold the slips and drop them in a hat or bowl. Then have the mother or father draw five (or some predetermined number). The fortune could take the form of best wishes or hopes for the new baby, such as those found in a Chinese fortune cookie. You might even team this activity with an Oriental menu or serve fortune cookies.

Babelets   Read aloud to your guests some definitions of things unique to babies (see below or think up your own). Ask them to coin a word for each definition.

Examples:
Dirty diapers—"oofers"
Pablum on baby's chin—"geedum"

Try these:
The mess on baby's tray when he's finished lunch _____ .
The smell of sour milk on baby's T-shirt _____ .
Baby food spinach and carrots. mixed together _____ .
The lint between baby's toes _____ .
Baby's hiccups _____ .

Mother Murphy Is Alive and Well   Read a few bits of wisdom excerpted from *Mother Murphy's Law* by Bruce Lansky. Encourage guests to make up their own sage bits of wisdom and record them in a notebook for the guest of honor to take home.
Examples:

Sure Fire Sex Determination
1. If most of the baby shower gifts you receive are blue, your baby will be a girl.
2. If most of the baby shower gifts you receive are pink, your baby will be a boy.
3. If most of the baby shower gifts you receive are lavender, your friends are gay.

The Sanitary Solution
1. When your first baby drops her pacifier, you sterilize it and wash the baby.
2. When your second child drops his pacifier, you pick it up off the floor, wipe it off on your shirt, and pop it back into his mouth.
3. When your third child drops her pacifier, you let the dog fetch it for her.

Baby Record Book Boredom
1. You record every little thing your firstborn does.
2. You record only your second child's birthdays.
3. You wouldn't recognize your third child in a police lineup.

The Teething Tenet
If the baby had a tooth for every time his parents said, "He's so fussy, he must be cutting a tooth," he'd be a crocodile.

Unstructured Activities

Who says a baby shower has to include any structured activity? Especially if the guests know each other well, let them entertain themselves, with the conversation flowing freely. At most, you might introduce one of the topics of conversation listed below. Provide ample food, comfortable surroundings, and maybe some music.

These "starters" can help you get a conversation rolling. Use them as a structured activity, or simply sneak them in informally. Either toss out a question to the whole group, or ask the views of one guest at a time. Discuss:

*   The way times have changed, especially regarding child-rearing. (Discussion could include discipline, developmental theories, baby equipment, doctors, etc.)
*   The funniest thing your baby ever did.
*   The most frustrating part of being a new parent.
*   The best or worst advice for a new parent.
*   The best or worst experience you ever had as a parent.
*   The best or worst experience you ever had when growing up.
*   Your baby's first words. (Read the following definitions excerpted from *Baby Talk*, by Bruce Lansky, to get started.)
    Fan fish (fan' fish) sandwich: syn. samich, sammy
    Gankey (gayng' kee) blanket: syn. bankey, blankey, coe, coo, eee, naney
    Mefawdow (mee fah dow') exp. "I fell down."

Nur-noos (nur' nooz) noodle; syn. getties, noodo, noods, noos, oodo

Oop (oop) n. soup

Tankoo (tan'koo) exp. "Thank you."; syn. tattoo

Umtoo (um too') exp. "I want some too."; syn. mememe-meme

Yitto (yi' toh) adj. little; syn. witto

- Interesting traditions from around the world. See Chapter Six of this book.

Prizes

The best prizes are those that are useful but a little special, not strictly utilitarian. It's better to spend a little more on fewer, but nicer, prizes than to go for a quantity of useless items. Keep your guest list in mind when choosing the prizes. Remember that even within a tight group of friends, tastes can vary dramatically. And since you have no idea who will win any particular prize, stay with fairly neutral colors and middle-of-the-road designs. Some suggestions for universally well-received prizes follow.

fun note/message pads or Post-it notes

shopping list pads

note cards or stationery

mugs (especially those with fun designs, like hearts or rainbows)

candy

small green plants in pots

bubblebath

refrigerator magnets

inexpensive paper foil napkin rings

heart-shaped ice cube trays (or other fun shapes)

magnetic picture frames

other plastic picture frames

coasters

padded hangers

fancy recipe cards

useful kitchen gadgets

fancy soaps

hand lotion

guest towels

pretty paper napkins and plates
cocktail napkins
a six-pack of beer or a bottle of wine
unusual pens
pocket organizers
mixed nuts
fancy office supplies such as gold or
    multi-colored paper clips
golf tees

fishing lures
tennis balls
plastic organizers (available in hard-
    ware stores, they come in various
    sizes to hold hardware, office
    supplies, sewing supplies and
    fishing tackle)
selected tidbits of imported foods
    from the supermarket

Chapter Five **Buying the Baby Gift**

The principal purpose of having a shower, aside from having a good time and offering moral support to the parents-to-be, is to ease some of the financial strain on the new family. Gifts of needed clothing, linens, and equipment will be much appreciated by any new parents—no matter what their budget.

Selecting the right gift can be great fun. It can be a real headache, too, especially if you are not sure of what the new parents want. Don't hesitate to check first with them. We've even provided a "wish list" (see page 77) to make it easy.

Most gifts fall into one of two categories: strictly practical items, or the "little luxuries." It's usually safe to buy the basics, because these are things every baby needs (undershirts, sleepers, booties, bibs, receiving blankets, crib sheets and so on). But the new parents might have received all these items from a friend who has older children, or at an earlier shower. So even when buying these "surefire" gifts, you may want to check with them first.

If the new parents have a good supply of the basics, you might want to get them something their baby doesn't absolutely need. The gift still might be useful, but a trifle frivolous. A handcrafted wall hanging with the baby's name and vital statistics on it would be a luxury, but useful in converting a spare bedroom into a real nursery. But do be careful: What if the parents receive six of these? Or, what if the pretty pastels you loved don't exactly harmonize with the bright, primary colors of the nursery that the parents have so carefully designed?

In short, baby shower gifts are bound to be appreciated. But you can help the new parents most with a little planning. As the host of a shower, you can play an important role. Let your guests know what the new parents would like, so that they can be "showered" with what they need most.

Tip: Ask guests to write a short description of their gift on the back of their gift card, to minimize the chance of a mix-up, and help the person who is recording gifts at the party.

Practical Gift Suggestions

Besides just listing the various items you can buy and their approximate price ranges, here are some ideas for fun, yet practical, gifts. Most of these ideas work well when several people are giving a group gift.

- Heap a diaper bag, diaper pail, baby bathtub or other larger gift with individually wrapped, small "treasures." The "treasures" might relate to the container. Try filling the diaper bag with diapers, fancy pins, baby powder, plastic pants and other related goodies. Fill the bathtub with a hooded towel, baby washcloths, castile soap (this mild, lightly scented soap is available in drugstores in animal shapes) and a rubber duckie. Wrapping each small gift individually prolongs the fun.
- If you want to buy something practical, yet want to add a little flair, combine plain undershirts, bibs, socks or plastic pants with one or two fancier versions for fun.
- If the mother has a definite decorating scheme or if she has a preferred pattern for linens and accessories, consider pooling funds with several other guests to buy a matching ensemble of crib sheets, comforter, bumper pad and diaper stacker. It's much more fun if the recipient doesn't have to exchange gifts or feel "stuck" with mismatched items.

Below are some ideas for gifts within general price categories. The price you actually pay will vary, depending on the store and the brand you choose.

Sales will make a difference. Often you can find baby clothing from the season just past on sale. It's fine to buy these outfits. The baby will fit them next year if you buy them large enough. In fact, often the gifts new parents need most are clothing items for sizes larger than 12 months.

We've marked "can't miss" items in the list below with an asterisk. These are the things almost every baby needs lots of.

Under $5

Booties*

T-shirts*

Socks

Tights

Hair "jewelry" (with velour or snap attachments)

Plastic pants

Hats (protection from sun or cold)

Mittens

"Baby wet" bell (alarm rings when diaper is wet)

Rattles

Bottles

Bottle cozy (keeps baby's meal warm)

Fancy diaper pins

Baby thermometer

Decorative switchplate cover

Diaper pail

Baby scissors

Bibs*

Tipper cup

Scooper bowl

Hangers

Crib toys

Feeding spoon/bent spoon

Hooded towel/washcloths*

Bathtub

Toothbrush

Baby powder, oil, soap, shampoo

Safety items: doorknob covers, outlet plugs, drawer locks and shockguards

Stroller bag

Waterproof lap pads

Receiving blanket*

Insulated bottle carrier (keeps formula warm)

$5 to $10

Cardigan sweater
Hooded sweater* (back zippers are
    easiest for putting on and
    taking off)
Sleeper
Stretch terry suit*
Gown
Grow bag/grow sleeper*
Tights (lace or printed design)
Jogging suit*
Sunsuit
Saque set
Creeper
Hat
Bunting bag
Shoes (baby versions of big-kid shoes,
    in gift box)
Switchplate covers
Nursery jar set
Hangers
Crib toys
Picture frame
Bank
Fancy cover bib
Sectioned warmer dish with suction
    cup
Baby food grinder
Plate/cup set
Feeding spoon (stainless steel)
Feeding set: feeding spoon, small
    fork, small spoon

Portable high chair
Hooded bath towel*/washcloths*
Baby bathtub
Sponge bath cushion
Potty chair
Crib sheet* (knit, cotton or flannel—
    look for prints)
Waterproof crib pads*
Blanket*
Quilt
Diaper stacker
Car seat/infant seat cover
Mattress pad
Receiving blanket*
Shawl
Fancy plastic pants
Musical toys
Plush animals
Bank
Grow chart
Jewelry
Take-along changing pad*
Nursery pad (for changing tables)
Nurser kit (bottles, nipples, bottle brush)
Safety ring (for sitting baby in big bathtub)
Place setting (cup, spoon, divided dish)
Revolving baby food organizer
Cloth diapers
Safety gate
Safety cuff/harness (keeps toddlers at hand

$10-$20

Body suit
Stretch terry coveralls*
Overalls
Jumpsuit
Sweater set
Jogging suit*
Sunsuit
Shortalls
Creepers*
Diaper set*
Pram suit
Dress
Gift shoes
Nursery lamp
Nursery jar set
Picture frame
Place setting (cup, spoon,
    divided dish)
Silver spoons, rattles
Potty chair
Baby scale
Designer sheets
Blanket

Quilt/comforter
Shawl
Zipper quilt* (converts from a com-
    forter to a sleeping bag)
Appliqued pillow with music box
Crib bumpers
Diaper stacker
Car seat/infant seat covers
Frontpack
Diaper bag
Carry bed/portable bed
Car seat
Toys*
Booster chair
Books:
    record book
    photo album
Grow chart
Bank
Jewelry
Revolving baby food organizer
Three-piece place setting of plastic,
    stainless or stoneware dishes

$20-$30-$40

Car seat*	Frontpack
Coveralls/jumpsuit	Diaper bag
Sweater set	Umbrella stroller
Creepers	Walker
Snowsuit	Carry/travel bed
Fancy dress	Plush animal
Nursery lamp	Swing
Hanging mobile	Play yard
Musical wall hanging	Silver bank
Johnny Jump-up	Jewelry
Picture frame	Infant seat
China place setting	Child's rocker
High chair	Crib mattress
Comforter	Intercom/nursery monitor
Crib bumper	Teddy bear that plays "in-the-womb" noises
Infant seat cover	Lambskin/lambskin hammock
Shawl	

"Big ticket" items

Often the most expensive baby items are the hardest to come by. They're things the parents really want or need, but perhaps can't afford. (Or, can't afford the quality they would like.)

At the top of the list is furniture. "Big ticket" items make good group gifts. Don't forget that it's doubly important, when buying furniture, to make sure the gift hasn't been acquired already!

When shopping for furniture, check for sturdiness. Joints should have metal reinforcements at stress points. Check high chairs for ease of operation. The trays on some new models can be operated with *one hand*—something it takes an experienced parent to really appreciate!

Crib
Bedroom furniture
Dressing table
Play yard
Crib mattress
High chair
Rocking chair for mother and baby

Intercom/monitor
Silver heirloom items
Silver spoons
Silver place setting
Gold ring, bracelet, locket
Starter savings account

Handcrafted and Unusual Gifts

If these items are thoughtfully planned with the recipient in mind, they are often the "hit" of the shower, destined to become heirlooms. You can either make them yourself, or purchase them at a boutique or a craft fair. Since many of them cannot be exchanged, be *sure* your gift is right before you commit yourself.

Baby bonnet made from a lace handkerchief (includes a card with instructions to snip a few threads and use on "baby's" wedding day for the bride to carry)
Bottle cozies in shapes
Wall hangings
Baby's name in large wooden letters
Personalized picture frames (hand-painted wood or cross-stitched on fabric)
Personalized quilts
Hand-knit sweaters
Christening gown
A "starter" for a collection—a *thimble, *demitasse cup, *silver spoon, *porcelain Beatrix Potter figurines or children's china, or *add-a-pearl necklace.

Coins minted in year of child's birth
Embroidered training pants
Quilted car seat cover
Fabric wall organizer with pockets
Hanging diaper carrier
Personalized porcelain baby bank
Handmade cloth baby's book
Diaper bag (folds out for changing pad, travel bed)
Kneekers (knee pads for crawlers)
Soft fabric rattles
Diaper dress-ups (pretty diaper covers)
Elegant baby basket (a real basket lined with ruffled baby quilt, blankets and pillow)
Framed newspaper front page and horoscope from the day the baby was born

Gifts for Mom and Dad

Don't forget the mother and father. If your budget can handle it, include a gift for the parents. A pair of theater tickets, a bottle of champagne and a certificate for an evening's baby sitting can be a real boost for overworked, over-tired new parents. For a special gift, a video cassette recorder (VCR) with a membership to a movie rental club will allow the parents to enjoy a night at the movies without the hassle of finding a babysitter.

Gifts for Mom

Sometimes new mothers experience a real let-down after the baby is born, due to physical changes, heavy workload, and loss of the limelight to the baby. Before the baby is born, people are constantly asking her how she feels, but afterward when she craves a little pampering, it's hard to compete with a new baby. Remembering the new mother with something just for her can give her a real lift. Here are some suggestions.

A pretty nightgown, robe or slippers
Perfume
Bath salts
Other lacy lingerie
Pretty stationery
Fancy hair accessories
Box of candy
Gift certificate for a new hairdo
A good book or magazine

A baby humor book
A pretty coffee mug
A cute sweatshirt or T-shirt with clever sayings about motherhood, e.g. "Supermom"
Jewelry
Relaxing record or tape
Something outrageous, like rhinestone-studded sunglasses

Gifts for Dad

In many cases, most of the baby shower gifts may be received and used by the new mother. That's all the more reason to remember the new father with a gift. After all, he's a part of the process too, yet often he feels left out. Some of these gifts are useful; others are just for fun.

Cigars (either real or bubblegum)
Film (for cameras, VCRs, movie
    cameras)
Blank tapes (for recording baby's first
    sounds)
Picture frame (for Dad's office)
Financial planner book

T-shirt that says "New Daddy" or
    "Super Dad" or "Because I'm
    the Daddy, That's Why!"
Barbecue apron that says "Super
    Dad"
A baby humor book

Survival kit—Sew or buy a canvas bag and include some or all of the following
for the trip to the hospital, his stay at home alone, and after the baby comes
home:

earplugs (drown out labor screams or
    baby crying)
granola bars, other snacks (so he can
    stay, without starving, while wife
    is in extended labor)
cue cards for labor coaching (breathe,
    don't breathe, push, don't push)
boxed beverages, such as Hi-C
parenting magazine (to while away
    the hours)
fast-food gift certificates

frozen dinners (for "home-cooked"
    meals while mom is in the
    hospital)
advice on how to cope with wife's
    post-partum depression
noseplugs for diaper changing
map of a baby (showing vital parts
    and their functions)
aspirin (self explanatory)
instant coffee

The mother-to-be can wrap up the following fun and practical helpers:

instructions on how to use (and how
    to find) the dishwasher, washer/
    dryer and other appliances.
phone numbers of doctor and
    hospital
mother-in-law's number
list of garbage day, etc.
pet feeding instructions

kitchen chart, locating pans, spices,
    utensils, dishes
If there are other kids, where their
    p.j.'s are, bedtimes, schedules for
    choir practice, football practice,
    carpool information and phone
    numbers

Plus, a "care package" including groceries he'll probably need:

peanut butter	beans and franks
macaroni and cheese	Spaghettios
instant coffee	TV dinners
bread	

Gifts for Siblings

If you know the expectant parents' other children well, you might provide a little gift for them as well. Older siblings sometimes feel left out and forgotten after the birth of a new brother or sister. Mom, Dad, and the new baby are showered with attention and gifts while they're parceled off to Grandma and Grandpa's house and told to stay out of the way. A gift from you or other shower guests can help ease that transistion from being the family's star to being a big brother or sister.

Fun T-shirts or sweatshirts with sayings like "Big Brother" or "Big Sister"

Quiet games that can be played alone (coloring books and crayons, hand-held games, puzzles)

Books geared to reading level and interests

An invitation for an afternoon or evening excursion (to the zoo, park or museum) or for a dinner to celebrate the birth. (The parents will thank you for this, too.)

Records or tapes (with a pair of headphones)

Books and Magazines

Both new parents are likely reading about their expected baby and parenthood. You can help by furnishing a magazine subscription or a lively book. Below are some of the best of both.

American Baby, 575 Lexington Ave., New York, NY 10022. (212)752-0775. Monthly; for expecting parents through those of one-year-olds.

Baby Talk, 185 Madison Ave., New York, NY 10016. (212)679-4400. Monthly; for expecting parents through those of two-year-olds.

Growing Child, 22 N. Second St., Lafayette, IN 47902. (317)423-2624. Monthly; for parents of newborns through those of six-year-olds.

Mothers Today, 441 Lexington Ave., New York, NY 10017. (212)867-4820. Bimonthly; for expecting parents through parents of four-year-olds.

Mothering, Box 2208, Albuquerque, NM 87103. (505)867-3110. Quarterly; for parents of newborns through those of five-year-olds, though some articles cover older children.

Parents Magazine, 685 Third Ave., New York, NY 10017. (212)878-8700. Monthly; for expecting parents through those of pre-teenagers.

Pediatrics for Parents, 176 Mount Hope Ave., Bangor, ME 04401. (207)942-6212. Monthly; for expecting parents through those of teenagers.

Practical Parenting Newsletter, 18326A Minnetonka Blvd., Deephaven, MN 55391. (612)475-1505. Bimonthly; for expecting parents through those of grade-schoolers.

Twins Magazine, P.O. Box 12045, Overland Park, KS 66212. (800)821-5533. Bimonthly; the only national magazine for the parents of twins.

Working Mother, 230 Park Ave., New York, NY 10169. (212)551-9412. Monthly; for parents of infants through pre-schoolers.

Child Development Brazelton, T. Berry. *Infants and Mothers* (Delacorte).
Caplan, Frank. *The First 12 Months of Life* (Bantam).
Hagstrom, Julie and Joan Morrill. *Games Babies Play* (A&W Visual Library).
Kelly, Dr. Paula. *Your Baby's First Three Years* (Meadowbrook).
Lansky, Bruce. *Baby Talk* (Meadowbrook).
Levy, Dr. Janine. *The Baby Exercise Book* (Pantheon).

Parenting Bard, Maureen. *Getting Organized for Your New Baby* (Meadowbrook).
Kelly, Marguerite and Elia S. Parsons. *Mother's Almanac* (Doubleday).
Lansky, Vicki. *Dear Babysitter* (Meadowbrook).
—*Practical Parenting Tips* (Meadowbrook).
Sullivan, S. Adams. *Father's Almanac* (Doubleday).

Grandparenting Sicora, Jean N. *Handbook for Beginning Grandparents.* (R.C. Press).

Food and Nutrition Eiger, M.D., Marvin S. and Sally Wendklos Olds. *The Complete Book of Breast-feeding* (Workman)
La Leche League. *The Womanly Art of Breastfeeding* (La Leche League).
Lansky, Vicki. *Feed Me! I'm Yours* (Meadowbrook).
Dana, Nancy and Anne Price, *Successful Breastfeeding* (Meadowbrook).

Medical Care Hart, M.D., Terril H. *The Parent's Guide to Baby and Child Medical Care* (Meadowbrook).
Pantell, M.D., Robert H. et al, *Taking Care of Your Child* (Addison Wesley).

Humor Barry, Dave. *Babies and Other Hazards of Sex.* (Rodale Press, Inc.)
Bloomingdale, Theresa. *I Should Have Seen It Coming When the Rabbit Died* (Bantam)
—*Murphy Must Have Been A Mother* (Bantam)
Bombeck, Erma. *The Grass is Always Greener Over the Septic Tank.*
—*I Lost it All in the Post-Natal Depression.*
—*Motherhood—The Second Oldest Profession.*
Johnston, Lynn. *David, We're Pregnant!* (Meadowbrook).
—*Hi Mom! Hi Dad!* (Meadowbrook).
—*Do They Ever Grow Up?* (Meadowbrook).
Lansky, Bruce. *Mother Murphy's Law* (Meadowbrook).

Gift Certificates

Some of the most memorable—and most meaningful—gifts are those not purchased in a store. Of these, one that's often overlooked is a gift of time. Why not give a booklet of certificates the new parents can redeem later, offering help with babysitting, meal preparation or housecleaning? Certificates can even simply offer advice or a sympathetic ear. The new parents realize there will be times when they'll need a hand. Knowing they can call on you can be a real sanity-saver.

You can fashion your own certificate booklet. Or, use the format in the Appendix. Copy the certificates (in the quantity you wish) on colored paper, then fill them out. Keep in mind the special interests—and needs—of your expectant friends. And be specific when filling them out so the recipient will feel free to redeem the "merchandise." For example, specify "three hours of babysitting" or "one afternoon of free babysitting" or several certificates rather than one certificate for "free babysitting."

In addition to the ideas above, consider certificates for:
- Parenting classes
- Decorating services or paint, wallpaper, other decorating supplies
- Oil or photo portrait of the baby
- Department store or children's store gift certificate
- Dusting, vacuuming
- Window-washing
- 1 room wallpaper hanging
- 1 free cup of tea and sympathetic ear
- 1 free grocery shopping trip
- 1 free ride to the pediatrician

"Wish List"

A "Wish List" can help ensure that the new parents receive more of the things they really need and want. The list can help you avoid duplication, too. Keep a master copy of this list (especially when a large number of guests are involved) to keep track of what has been purchased. Or, make copies of the completed list and include them when you mail the invitations. You will have to decide which works best for you.

Many of the items on this list are similar. They are included so that parents-to-be with definite preferences can be as specific as they want to be. The most useful information is the color scheme of the nursery, the preferred nursery design (if the parents have chosen one) and their preferred brand names for equipment. Even with this specific information, guests will probably purchase what they personally like; this list will serve mainly as a guideline.

Wish List

Preferred clothing colors: _____
Nursery color scheme: _____
Nursery pattern: _____

CLOTHING

Quantity Desired	Quantity Received	Item	Color/Pattern/Sizes
		Gown	
		Stretch terry coverall	
		Body suit	
		Cardigan sweater	
		Hooded sweater	
		Grow sleeper	
		Blanket sleeper	
		Undershirts	
		Coverall/jumpsuit	
		Creeper	
		Grow bag	
		Overall	
		Sweater set	
		Jog suit	
		Sunsuit	
		Shortall	
		Sacque set	
		Creeper	
		Diaper set	
		Sunhat	
		Bunting bag	
		Pram suit	

CLOTHING cont.

Quantity Desired	Quantity Received	Item	Color/Pattern/Sizes
		Snow suit	
		Warm hat	
		Mittens	
		Footsies/booties	
		Socks	
		Tights	
		T-shirts	
		Cloth diapers	
		Disposable diapers	
		Diaper liner	
		Plastic pants	
		Training pants	
		Diaper pins	
		Shoes	
		Dress	
		Dress suit	
		Christening dress	

NURSERY FURNITURE/EQUIPMENT

Quantity Desired	Quantity Received	Item	Brand/Style/Color/Pattern
		Lamp	
		Mobile	
		Switchplate cover	

NURSERY FURNITURE/EQUIPMENT cont.

Quantity Desired	Quantity Received	Item	Brand/Style/Color/Pattern
		Wall hanging	
		Diaper pail	
		Scissors	
		Nursery jar set	
		Pinholder	
		Crib toy	
		Johnny Jump-up	
		Picture frame	
		Nursery monitor/intercom	
		High chair	
		Potty chair	
		Baby scale	
		Sterilizer	
		Room vaporizer	
		Cradle	
		Crib	
		Umbrella stroller	
		Conventional stroller/carriage	
		Swing	
		Play yard	
		Safety gate	
		Walker	
		Carry bed	
		Infant seat	
		Car seat	
		Backpack/carrier	
		Seat cover	
		Changing table	
		Dresser	
		Booster chair	

NURSERY FURNITURE/EQUIPMENT cont.

Quantity Desired	Quantity Received	Item	Brand/Style/Color/Pattern
		Basket/linen	
		Feeding equipment	
		Nurser set	
		Bottles	
		Bottle brush	
		Nipples	
		Bib	
		Plastic bib	
		Food grinder	
		Scooper plate	
		Heated feeding dish	
		Tipper cup	
		Cup/dish set	
		Feeding spoon	
		Bent spoon	
		Silver spoon	
		Silver cup	
		Portable highchair	

BATH

Quantity Desired	Quantity Received	Item	Brand/Style/Color/Pattern
		Washcloth	
		Hand towel	
		Hooded towel	
		Portable bathtub	
		Sponge bath cushion	
		Bath toy	
		Toothbrush	
		Baby powder	
		Baby oil	
		Baby shampoo	
		Brush/comb	
		Baby thermometer	
		Zipper after-bath coverup	
		Bedding	
		Sheet	
		Waterproof matress cover	
		Waterproof lap pad	
		Blanket	
		Receiving blanket	
		Shawl	
		Quilt	
		Zipper quilt	
		Pillow	
		Crib bumper	

MISCELLANEOUS cont.

Quantity Desired	Quantity Received	Item	Brand/Style/Color/Pattern
		Crib/playpen toys	
		Development toys	
		Rockabye bear	
		Other	

BOOKS

Quantity Desired	Quantity Received	Item	Title Author
		Baby record book	
		Snapshot book	
		''Brag'' book	
		Cookbook	
		Babysitter instruction book	
		Baby calendar	
		Medical book	
		Parenting tips	
		Mother Goose	
		Humor book	
		Other	

MISCELLANEOUS

Quantity Desired	Quantity Received	Item	Brand/Style/Color/Pattern
		Pacifiers	
		Teeth	
		Grow chart	
		Music box	
		Bank	
		Christening jewelry	
		Musical toy	
		Doll	
		Plush animal	

Gift wrapping suggestions

- Instead of investing in expensive commercial gift wrap, buy an inexpensive rattle, a small, inexpensive stuffed toy or some hand-painted diaper pins. Wrap the gift in inexpensive tissue, then tie it with two or three colors of ribbon to make a "confetti" curled bow. Tie the extra gift into the bow. Or, wrap the gift in a receiving blanket (a pretty print would be best) and fasten it with cute diaper pins.

- Colorful gift bags are fun, and you can make your own. Wrap paper around a box a little larger than your gift, leaving the end open. Fasten with clear tape or rubber cement. Crease the edges. Slide the box out the open end and trim the top of the bag with pinking shears. Insert the gift. Punch two holes near the top of the bag, then thread your ribbon through and tie. You can also punch a hole in your gift card and hang it from the ribbon. That way your card won't get lost or mixed up with one from another gift.

- You can make a beautiful tissue paper flower to use for a bow. Cut six to eight layers of tissue paper into rectangles, eight by five inches. (You can vary the size to make larger bows, once you master the smaller ones.) Use just one color of tissue or several to match your package. Accordion-fold layers of tissue in one-inch folds, then trim like this:

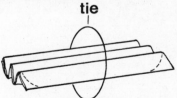

Attach a pipe cleaner around the center of the folded tissue, and twist it tightly to cinch the center. Fan out the accordion folds and gently pull the layers of "petals" out to form a flower.

Chapter Six Traditions From Around the World

Babies have been a fascinating topic of conjecture and conversation for centuries. It's fun to look at some of the beliefs, customs and stories that have been passed along through the generations. Some of these follow and might be fun to talk about at your shower. Your guests may have others to share as well.

American Folklore   Every time a star shoots, a baby is born in that direction.

To dream of fish means you'll have a baby.

To dream about fire means a girlfriend is pregnant.

If the baby's heartbeat is more than 140 beats per minute, it's a girl. If it's less than 140, it's a boy.

If a child cries at birth and lifts up one hand, he or she is born to command.

A gold coin placed in the hand of a new baby brings good luck. The coin should be saved for presentation to the child of the next generation.

If the baby smiles in its sleep, it is talking with angels.

A child born with two cowlicks will be bright.

Monday's child is fair of face,
Tuesday's child is full of grace,
Wednesday's child is sour and sad,
Thursday's child is merry and glad,
Friday's child is loving and giving,
Saturday's child must work for a living;
But the child born on the Sabbath Day
Is blithe and bonny and good and gay.

If a woman leaves a diaper under a bed in the home where she is visiting, there soon will be another birth at that house. Hence, the sayings: "Don't leave a diaper here"—when the hostess does not desire a child; and, "Somebody left a diaper"—after a child has been born.

A woman on the first visit to a newly born child should not hold it in her arms, for she will become a mother.

If a married woman is the first person to see a recently born infant, she will have the next child.

The woman who lays her coat or hat on a strange bed will have a baby.

If outgrown baby clothes are given away the mother will soon need them again.

To find a baby's pacifier means an approaching birth in the family.

If you go swimming the first day you are married you will have twins.

Count apple seeds to discover the number of your future children.

Blow a dandelion seed ball and the number of seeds left will show how many children you are going to have.

Count the veins branching out from the main vein in your wrist and that will be the number of children you are going to have.

Count the wrinkles in your forehead and you will know the number of your future children.

A poor man is certain to have many children.

A happily married couple will procreate good-looking children. If a husband and wife quarrel continually, their children will be ugly.

Twins run in every third generation.

The birth of a female proves that the woman is stronger than her husband.

When a male is born, the man has more strength than his wife.

At a baby shower, the guest whose gift is the seventh to be opened will be the next to have a baby.

Eskimo Customs

After the birth of an Eskimo male baby, a shaman will often place a small ivory carving of a whale in the child's mouth. It is believed this will influence the child to become a fine hunter. The shaman also beats a drum and sings to make the boy stouthearted and manly.

Formerly, among the Unalit Eskimo tribe, when a woman was confined with her first child she was considered unclean and put out in a tent or other shelter by herself for a period. (Fortunately, the custom is now becoming obsolete.)

Japanese Custom

To celebrate the arrival of a boy, the Japanese fly a fish kite from the house.

Chinese Custom

To celebrate the birth of a girl, the Chinese give red-dyed eggs.

English Folklore and Customs

In England, it was believed that during the time between birth and baptism, a child was particularly liable to be stolen by fairies, and have a changeling left in its place. To avert these perils, a piece of iron or some salt or the father's coat were put on the bedfoot; or the bed itself was "sained" by carrying a lighted torch or candle around it. The protective power of fire and salt against all forms of evil was believed to be very great.

Also, small pieces of cheese or bread, called "blithe meat," were scattered in and about the house for the fairies. The woman who carried the infant to the church for baptism also was supplied with bread and cheese to give to the first person she met on the way, in order to preserve the child from evil influences.

In some places, a pinch of salt was put in the baby's mouth on its first visit to another house.

In the North of England, the father's clothes were laid over a girl and the mother's petticoat over a boy to make the child attractive to the opposite sex.

German Customs and Folklore

It is believed in Germany that babies are delivered by storks, owls, crows and even, on the Baltic Sea island of Rugen, by swans.

In Swabia, children who want to have a little brother or sister place lumps of sugar outside on window sills to attract the stork.

In the Harz Mountains, little ones are told that a turkey scratches babies out of the gatepost.

Rocking an empty cradle will make a mother give birth to a sleepless baby.

Neighbors sometimes would bring the new mother a "schwatzei" or gossip-egg that is touched to the baby's mouth so he will learn to talk early.

In Bavaria, people still believe that if brothers and sisters are christened in the light of the same candle, they will always love each other, so it is important to pick a heavy candle for the first offspring's christening.

Jewish Custom

It was formerly common to plant a tree at the birth of a child, a cedar for a boy and a pine for a girl. When a couple married, their respective trees were cut down and used in the construction of the "huppah" or the bridal bower.

Swiss Custom

It is the practice to plant an apple tree at the birth of a boy and a pear or nut tree at that of a girl.

Swedish Custom

An addition to the family is frequently marked by the planting of a "tree of destiny" in his or her home.

Variations of this practice persist in other parts of the world; often the fate of the tree is said to parallel that of the child.

Chinese Custom

The evil eye is attracted to beauty. Therefore, the assocation of the evil eye with the praising of babies and young children has led to the custom of addressing them by derogatory names and resenting any use of flattery by admiring relatives and friends. In China, children are often nicknamed, "dog," "hog" or "flea" to minimize the danger of the evil eye.

Indian Custom

To avoid the evil eye, a male child may be called "dunghill," "grasshopper" or "beggar" and a female child "blind," "dusty" or "fly." Today, we are following that old practice when we address our children affectionately as "scamp" or "little rascal."

Albanian Customs and Folklore

In the 1800s, it was common to plaster a lump of mud, softened in water previously prepared with magical charms, on a newborn baby's forehead to protect it from the evil eye. More recently, Albanian women have gathered after a childbirth carrying gifts of eggs, one of which was broken over the face of the baby. Defacing a child in these ways rendered it less attractive, and, therefore, less likely to invite an envious eye.

Appendix

Directions On Making Cards

All of the cards in the Appendix are designed to fit into 4-1/2″ X 5-1/2″ envelopes, which are available at most stationery and department stores. Many shops have color coordinated envelopes and paper, so that you can make the invitations out of pink paper and match them with blue envelopes, or use a color scheme that fits the theme you have chosen for the party.

Designs can be photocopied on to the paper, depending on the type of copying machine available to you, or they can be traced.

Single-sided Notes Below are directions for making single-sided note cards with designs on the front and information inside the design or on the back. For single-sided cards, with shower information on the front, you can use the back of the card as the mailing side, filling in your address and the guests' mailing addresses. You save the expense of purchasing envelopes, but use heavy stock paper so it doesn't get damaged in the mail.

STORK ON FRONT →

↙ WRITE INFO ON BACK

Folded Notes   Following the directions below, trace or copy your chosen card design on one quarter of a 8-1/2" X 11" piece of paper. Then fill in the shower information on the quarter across from it (see diagram). When you fold it, you'll have a card with a design on the front and the information inside.

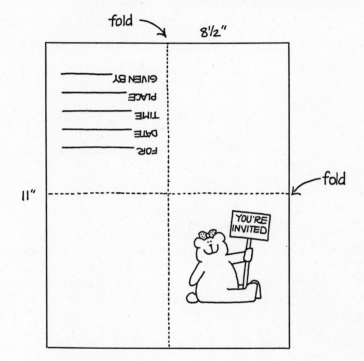

Remember   When creating your own invitations, be sure to include all of the pertinent information:
- name(s) of the guest(s) of honor
- the date, time and address of the shower
- your name, address and telephone number
- whether or not you want regrets only or RSVP's
- whether the party is for women only or for couples and men

Diapers

Cut a piece of stationery in a triangle shape and fasten with a small, gold safety pin, as shown here. Write the shower information (date, time, guest(s) of honor, address, telephone number) on the inside. Be sure that the folded triangle fits in the envelopes you have chosen for your invitations.

INVITATION

FOLD

FOLD

You're Invited to a
BABY SHOWER

Time: _____

For: _____
Date: _____
Place: _____

Given by: _____

FOLD

This name tag can be made by cutting a white or colored triangle of paper and folding (according to diagram). The "diaper" should be fastened with a safety pin that guests can use to attach the name tag. (For door prizes, add a small dollop of mustard in a few name tags. Guests receiving "dirty" diapers win door prizes.)

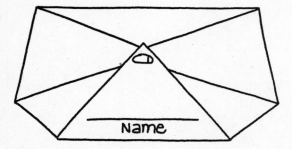

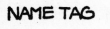

NAME TAG

FOLD

FOLD

Stork

Trace or copy this stork shape on to 4-1/4″ X 5-1/4″ paper and write the shower information on the front, inside the stork's body. Or, depending on the copier available to you, photocopy the stork shape on to the invitation paper.

If you want a card that opens, see the directions on page 92 of the Appendix.

INVITATION

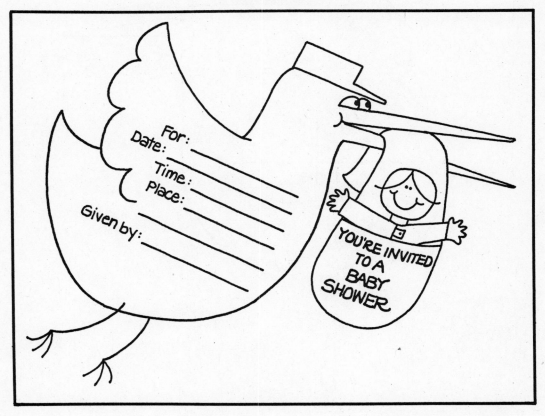

For:
Date: _____
Time: _____
Place: _____
Given by: _____

YOU'RE INVITED
TO A
BABY
SHOWER

Trace and cut this stork shape out of the same paper you used for the invitations, or out of white or pastel construction paper.

NAME TAG

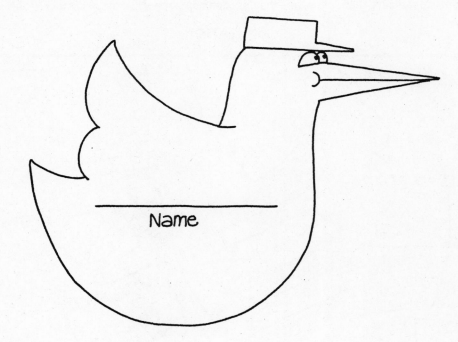

Name

Teddy Bears

Trace or copy this cheery bear on to note paper (see directions for single side and folded cards on page 92 of the Appendix).

INVITATION

WRITE INFO INSIDE

Trace or copy these bears on tan or pastel construction paper. If you're feeling creative, add real ribbon, sequins or other decorations.

NAME TAGS

Name

Name

Baby Cradle

Trace or copy the outline of this baby cradle (you can eliminate the balloons if you want) on to construction paper or card paper and write the information about the shower in the cradle shape.

Or trace or copy the design on to note cards or 8-1/2" X 11" paper (see directions for one-sided and folded note cards on page 92) and fill in the shower information.

INVITATION

YOU'RE INVITED TO A   BABY   SHOWER

For: _____
Date: _____ Time: _____
Place: _____
_____
Given by:
_____
_____

Trace or copy this cradle shape for your name tags. For a special touch, add a piece of fabric for the quilt or color the baby's face with colored pens.

NAME TAG

Name

Trees

Photocopy or trace this tree outline for your shower invitations. (See directions on page 92 of the Appendix for making one-sided or folded invitations.)

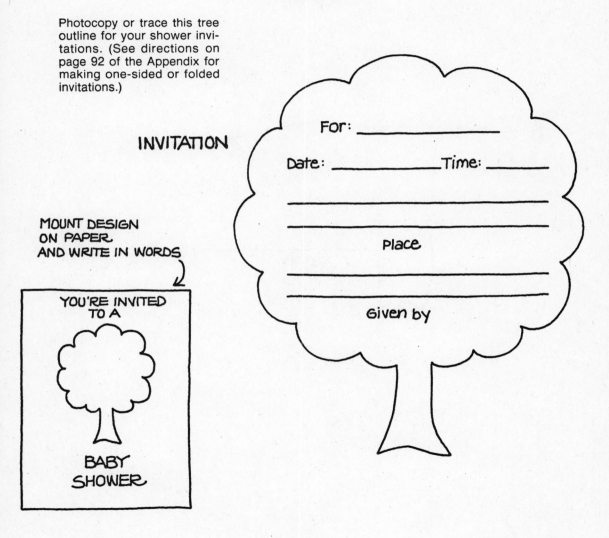

INVITATION

For: _____

Date: _____ Time: _____

_____

_____

Place

_____

Given by

MOUNT DESIGN
ON PAPER
AND WRITE IN WORDS

YOU'RE INVITED
TO A

BABY
SHOWER

Trace this leaf shape and cut it out of colored construction paper (green, or red, yellow and orange) for name tags for your tree theme.

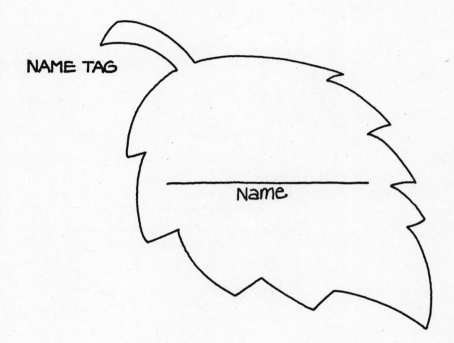

NAME TAG

Name

Cowboy Hats

You can copy or trace this invitation design. One idea is to trace the cowboy hat outline and cut it out of brown construction paper, then glue it to the front of a folded note. You can add a ribbon for the hat band and a feather decoration. Or, copy the front and add pertinent information on the inside of a folded note. (See page 92 in the Appendix for directions to make cards.)

INVITATION

YOU'RE INVITED
TO A
**BABY
SHOWER**

You can trace the same cowboy hat shape on to brown construction paper and use it for name tags at the party.

NAME TAG

Name

Twins

Here's a pattern to use for making a special invitation for a "twins" shower. Start with a 5-1/2" X 8-1/2" sheet of paper folded as shown below. Trace the baby shape and cut it out.

Once you have the twins shape cut out, fold the invitation once at the point where the hands and feet meet (see diagram below). Write the shower information across the babies on the inside.

PATTERN TO CUT

HOW TO FOLD PAPER SIZE 5¼" X 10"
TO MAKE TWIN PAPER DOLLS

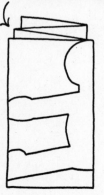

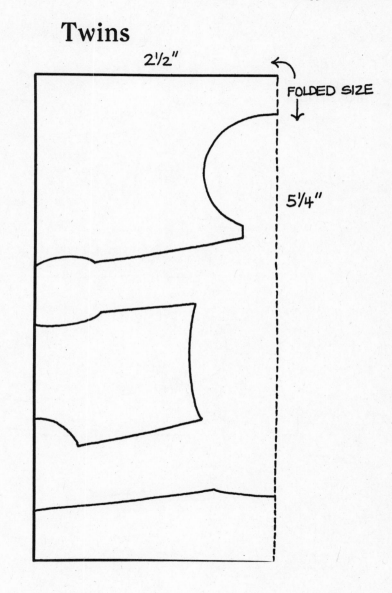

2½"

FOLDED SIZE

5¼"

INVITATION

FRONT →

BACK →

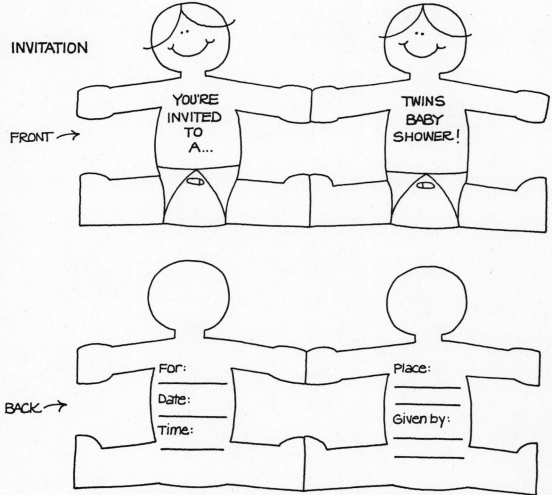

For the twins' name tags, trace or copy the shape below or copy it on to construction paper, cut in rectangles. Provide a line for guests to write in their names.

NAME TAG

Grapevine

Copy this grapevine design for either a note or a folded card. (See directions on how to make one-sided notes or folded cards on page 92 of the Appendix.) Write pertinent shower information on the back or inside the folded card.

INVITATION

We heard it through the grapevine...

You're Invited to a
BABY
SHOWER

↖ WRITE INFO ON THE BACK

Trace this grapevine design and cut it out of construction paper for name tags.

NAME TAG

Name

Good Deed Certificates

Copy as many ''Good Deed'' certificates as you want, filling in the blanks with useful services you can provide for the new mother and baby (such as ''three hours of baby-sitting,'' or ''one emergency baby-sitting call, redeemable anytime'' or ''one free drive to and from the doctor's office''). Once you've made as many copies as you want, staple or clip them in a book for a present.

Name Tag Designs

Trace or copy these baby-related items and add them to guests' name tags (without letting them see what they are) to play the name tag game listed on page 56. Guests should ask other party guests ''yes'' and ''no'' questions about the design on their name tag until they guess it correctly. This game helps shower guests meet one another and gets lively conversations started.

Name

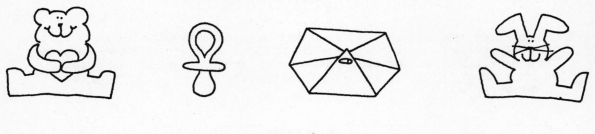

Memo

Here's an office memo invitation idea to use when you're planning an office baby shower. Be sure to make your "memo" look slightly different than the company's standard memo so that people will sit up and take notice of the invitation.

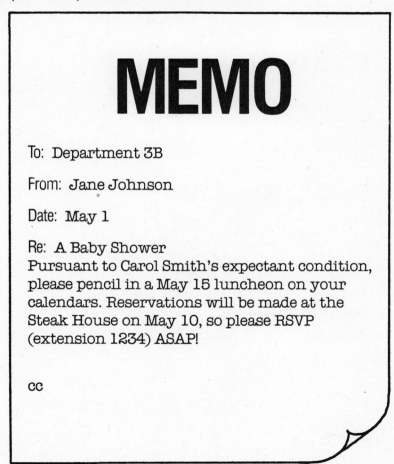

MEMO

To: Department 3B

From: Jane Johnson

Date: May 1

Re: A Baby Shower
Pursuant to Carol Smith's expectant condition, please pencil in a May 15 luncheon on your calendars. Reservations will be made at the Steak House on May 10, so please RSVP (extension 1234) ASAP!

cc

Office Memo (Phone Message)

To _____

Subject _____

IT'S A PARTY!

For _____

of _____ Department

at _____

_____

Date _____   Time _____

RSVP	Regrets only	

Message _____

_____

_____

Contact _____

Extension _____

Copy this telephone message slip invitation for an office shower. Be sure to use paper that looks somewhat different than the telephone message slips your company uses. Otherwise, people might mistake it for a real telephone message and overlook the invitation!

Baby Profile Form

As each guest arrives, choose a category from below and ask them to give you a color, number, etc. to use to fill in the blank. Don't let them know what their suggestions are being used for. If you have more guests than categories, make up a few of your own and add them to the form.

Baby Profile Date of party _____

First name _____

height

_____

weight

_____

hair _____

eyes _____

male _____

female _____

occupation

_____

_____

hobbies

_____

_____

favorite foods

_____

_____

_____

_____

Cartoons

Copy these captionless cartoons and post them, with pens and pencils, at the party. Display them together or scatter them around. Invite your guests to write their own captions. At the end of the party, collect them and present them to the new parents.

Baby Pool Forms

Copy the baby pool forms here and cut them apart (be sure to provide enough forms so that guests can bet more than once if they want). If you are collecting money for each bet, place the forms on a table next to a piggy bank with directions on how much it costs per bet and where the money will go. Be sure to mention the prize for the winner.

date of birth _____
time of birth _____
length _____ weight _____
sex _____
your name _____

Baby Pool

date of birth _____
time of birth _____
length _____ weight _____
sex _____
your name _____

Baby Pool

Baby Trivia Game

Play this "Baby Trivia" game to get all of the guests at the shower involved and talking. You can divide the group into teams and take turns asking questions; or, ask questions of the group at large. The first person to answer correctly gets a point. Or, make up your own rules.

Baby Trivia Quiz

 1 Who was the first professional baseball player to father a test tube baby? Hint: he is a Cy Young Award winner.
Answer: Mike Flanagan

 2 Best known as "John Boy," he is the father of triplets. Who is he?
Answer: Richard Thomas

3 What do Alice Cooper, Glen Campbell, Aretha Franklin, and Lou Rawls have in common?
Answer: They are the children of ministers.

 4 What are Prince Charles and Princess Diana's sons' first names?
Answer: William and Henry

 5 Who wrote "Mommy Dearest"?
Answer: Christina Crawford

 6 Florence Henderson and Robert Reed were the parents in what TV situation comedy?
Answer: "The Brady Bunch"

 7 What movie depicts Dudley Moore as the harried husband of two pregnant wives?
Answer: "Micki and Maude"

8 Who was the first test-tube baby?
Answer: Louise Joy Brown

 9 What recent motion picture comedy portrayed the male partner in a marriage as a full-time nurturer and parent?
Answer: "Mr. Mom"

 10 Who is "Sweet Baby James"?
Answer: Singer James Taylor's son.

11 What contemporary singer sang, "You've Got To be Somebody's Baby"?
Answer: Jackson Browne

 12 What was the real name of "Baby Snooks" (of old time radio fame)?
Answer: Fanny Brice

 13 What two female screen legends portrayed the main characters in "Whatever Happened to Baby Jane?"
Answer: Bette Davis and Joan Crawford

14 What baby was "brought up" in "Bringing up Baby"—the movie starring Cary Grant?
Answer: A leopard

 15 What organization is the world-wide proponent of breastfeeding?
Answer: La Leche League

 16 What was the name of Gloria and Mike's baby in TV's "All in the Family"?
Answer: Joey

 17 What TV morning news show host is the mother of twins?
Answer: Jane Pauley

 18 Twins also "light up the life" of what singer?
Answer: Debby Boone

 19 His father Woody was a famous folk balladeer and he followed in those footsteps with songs like "Alice's Restaurant." Who is he?
Answer: Arlo Guthrie

20 Susan Sarandon and Brooke Shields played mother and daughter in what film?
Answer: "Pretty Baby"

 21 Tatum and Griffin are the children of what screen star?
Answer: Ryan O'Neal

 22 Who is actor James McArthur's actress mother?
Answer: Helen Hayes

 23 What recent Broadway musical featured Mickey Rooney and Ann Miller?
Answer: "Sugar Babies"

 24 Who played the mother in "The Waltons"?
Answer: Michael Learned

 25 Where was Mork born?
Answer: Ork

 26 Blanche Baker recently starred in "Lolita" on Broadway, 20 years after her mother created waves in "Baby Doll." Who is Baker's mother?
Answer: Carroll Baker

 27 What television actress waged a highly publicized battle to nurse her baby on the set?
Answer: Lynn Redgrave

 28 What TV show portrayed the foibles of a large family and starred Dick Van Patten as the father?
Answer: "Eight is Enough"

 29 What famous green frog, friend to millions of children, celebrated his 30th birthday in 1985?
Answer: Kermit the Frog

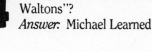 **30** What pint-size star won everyone's heart in the remake of "The Champ"?
Answer: Ricky Schroeder

31 What daughters of presidents are novelists?
Answer: Margaret Truman and Patti Davis

 32 Richard Simon of Simon and Schuster publishing group is the father of what famous singer?
Answer: Carly Simon

 33 Who wrote, "The child is father of the man; and I could wish my days to be bound to each by natural piety."
Answer: William Wordsworth

34 Who said, "The more people have studied different methods of bringing up children the more they have come to the conclusion that what good mothers and fathers instinctively feel like doing for their babies is the best after all."
Answer: Dr. Benjamin Spock in "The Common Sense Book of Baby and Child Care."

 35 Who said, "Familiarity breeds contempt and children"?
Answer: Mark Twain

 36 Who wrote the play, "The Children's Hour"?
Answer: Lillian Hellman

37 Who wrote, "Between the dark and the daylight, when the night is beginning to lower, Comes a pause in the day's occupations, That is known as the Children's Hour"?
Answer: Henry Wadsworth Longfellow

 38 Who wrote "Motherhood, the Second Oldest Profession"?
Answer: Erma Bombeck

 39 In what country is it against the law to spank your child?
Answer: Sweden

 40 Who wrote "The Tales of Peter Rabbit"?
Answer: Beatrix Potter

41 Who wrote "A Child's Garden of Verses"?
Answer: Robert Louis Stevenson

42 What is Dr. Seuss's real name?
Answer: Theodore Geisel

 43 Candice Bergen and her husband, a French film director, recently had a baby. Who is Bergen's husband?
Answer: Louis Malle

 44 Ryan O'Neal and what blonde beauty recently had a baby?
Answer: Farrah Fawcett

 45 What film actress is the foster mother to several handicapped and foreign-born children? Hint: She's Woody Allen's companion.
Answer: Mia Farrow

46 Name the Italian educator whose educational methods stress creativity and less restricted learning?
Answer: Maria Montessori

47 Who created the Cabbage Patch Kids?
Answer: Xavier Roberts

 48 What's the name of the program that pairs senior citizens with special children?
Answer: Foster Grandparent Program.

 49 Eight-month-old Parks Bonifay made the Guinness record book as the youngest person to do what on water?
Answer: Water ski

 50 What child star of the '30s sang "On The Good Ship Lollipop"?
Answer: Shirley Temple

Baby Sex Determination Form

Use the form below to tally up the scores from the Baby Sex Determination Test on page 58 to determine if the baby will be a boy or a girl.

Sex Determination

Test Form

1. Girl _____ Boy _____
2. Girl _____ Boy _____
3. Girl _____ Boy _____
4. Girl _____ Boy _____
5. Girl _____ Boy _____
6. Girl _____ Boy _____
7. Girl _____ Boy _____
8. Girl _____ Boy _____
9. Girl _____ Boy _____
10. Girl _____ Boy _____
11. Girl _____ Boy _____

First-Year Baby Care

by Paula Kelly, M.D.

The practical guide that shows you how to take care of your baby for the first twelve months. Easy-to-use format, over 100 photos and illustrations. Practical yet thorough and up-to-date.
(S & S Ordering #: 54497-7) $5.95

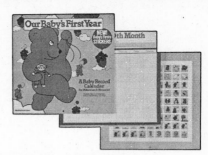

Our Baby's First Year

Now with 81 "Baby's-Firsts" Stickers

A nursery calendar with 13 undated months for recording "big events" of baby's first year. Each month features animal characters, baby care tips and development information. The 81 "baby's-firsts" stickers add color and convenience.
(S & S Ordering #: 54486-1) $7.95

Baby & Child Medical Care

by Terril H. Hart, M.D.

A first aid and home treatment guide that shows parents how to handle over 150 common childhood illnesses in a step-by-step illustrated format.
(S & S Ordering #: 54470-5) $7.95

Successful Breastfeeding

by Nancy Dana and Anne Price

A practical illustrated guide for nursing mothers; tells how to overcome the most common problems and complications.
(S & S Ordering #: 55611-8) $8.95

Baby Talk

by Bruce Lansky

A guide for helping your baby learn to talk and for understanding your baby's talk. Includes language development; games, rhymes, songs, books; plus a dictionary of baby talk.
(S & S Ordering #: 60570-4) $4.95

Feed Me! I'm Yours

by Vicki Lansky

Parents love this easy-to-use economical guide for making fresh, pure baby food at home. Over 200 recipes for sneaking nutrition into infants, toddlers, and tots. Includes a valuable list of finger foods, seasonal fun foods, and birthday party ideas.
(S & S Ordering #: 62278-1) $6.95

Pregnancy, Childbirth and the Newborn

by Penny Simkin, R.P.T.; Janet Whalley, R.N., B.S.N. and Ann Keppler, R.N., M.N.

Developed by the Childbirth Education Association of Seattle, this book is the most complete, up-to-date, illustrated guide to pregnancy and childbirth available.
(S & S Ordering #: 54498-5) $9.95

Mother Murphy's Law

by Bruce Lansky

A collection of Murphy-style laws that detail the perils and pitfalls of parenthood.
(S & S Ordering #: 62274-9) $2.95

Qty.	Order #	Book Title	Author	Price
_____	54470-5	Baby and Child Medical Care	Hart, T.	$ 7.95
_____	60570-4	Baby Talk	Lansky, B.	$ 4.95
_____	62276-5	Best Baby Shower Book, The	Cooke, C.	$ 4.95
_____	54463-2	Best Baby Name Book, The	Lansky, B.	$ 3.95
_____	54476-4	David, We're Pregnant!	Johnston, L.	$ 3.95
_____	54477-2	Dear Babysitter	Lansky, V.	$ 7.95
_____	54588-4	Dear Babysitter Refill Pad	Lansky, V.	$ 2.95
_____	54464-0	Discipline Without Shouting or Spanking	Wyckoff/Unell	$ 4.95
_____	54478-0	Do They Ever Grow Up?	Johnston, L.	$ 3.95
_____	62278-1	Feed Me! I'm Yours	Lansky, V.	$ 6.95
_____	54497-7	First-Year Baby Care	Kelly, P.	$ 5.95
_____	63066-0	Free Stuff for Kids	FSFK Editors	$ 3.95
_____	62275-7	Getting Organized For Your New Baby	Bard, M.	$ 4.95
_____	54481-0	Grandma's Favorites Photo Album	Meadowbrook	$ 6.50
_____	54482-9	Hi Mom! Hi Dad!	Johnston, L.	$ 3.95
_____	62274-9	Mother Murphy's Law	Lansky, B.	$ 2.95
_____	54543-4	My First Five Years Record Book	Meadowbrook	$11.95
_____	54484-5	My First Year Calendar	Meadowbrook	$ 6.95
_____	54485-3	My First Year Photo Album	Meadowbrook	$14.95
_____	54486-1	Our Baby's First Year Calendar	Meadowbrook	$ 7.95
_____	54487-X	Practical Parenting Tips	Lansky, V.	$ 6.95
_____	54498-5	Pregnancy, Childbirth and the Newborn	Simkin/Whalley	$ 9.95
_____	54467-5	Self-Esteem for Tots to Teens	Anderson, G.	$ 4.95
_____	55611-8	Successful Breastfeeding	Dana/Price	$ 8.95
_____	55692-4	10,000 Baby Names	Lansky, B.	$ 2.95
_____	54495-0	You & Me Baby	Regnier, S.	$ 8.95

Please send me copies of the books checked above. I am enclosing $ _____ which covers the full amount per book shown above plus $1.00 for postage and handling for the first book and $.50 for each additional book. (Add $2.00 to total for postage and handling for books shipped to Canada. Overseas postage and handling will be billed. MN residents add 6% sales tax.) Allow up to four weeks for delivery. Quantity discounts available upon request.

Send check or money order to Meadowbrook, Inc. No cash or C.O.D.s, please.

For purchases over $10.00, you may use VISA or MasterCard (order by mail or phone). For these orders we need information below.
Charge to: ☐ **VISA**   ☐ **MasterCard**

Account # _____

Expiration Date _____

Card Signature _____

Send Book(s) to:

Name _____

Address _____

City _____ State _____ Zip _____

Mail order to: Book Orders, Meadowbrook, Inc., 18318 Minnetonka Blvd., Deephaven, MN 55391, Phone orders: (612) 473-5400